Holy Places

Holy Places

TRUE STORIES OF FAITH AND MIRACLES FROM LATTER-DAY TEMPLES

WRITTEN AND ILLUSTRATED BY
CHAD S. HAWKINS

DESERET
BOOK

SALT LAKE CITY, UTAH

The images of temples included in this volume are available as fine-art prints from Deseret Book Company and other distributors of LDS products. For more information, contact Chad Hawkins Art, Inc., by telephone at 801-544-3434; by FAX at 801-544-4122; by mail at P.O. Box 292, Layton, UT 84041; or by email at artist@integrity.com

If you have documented stories regarding temples in your area, e-mail them to the author at artist@integrity.com

Library of Congress Cataloging-in-Publication Data

Hawkins, Chad S., 1971–
  Holy places : true stories of faith and miracles from Latter-day temples /
Chad Hawkins.
    p. cm.
  Includes index.
  ISBN 1-59038-545-4 (hardbound : alk. paper)
  1. Mormon temples. I. Title.
  BX8643.T4H385 2006
  246'.9589332—dc22   2005033837

Printed in the United States of America
R. R. Donnelley and Sons, Crawfordsville, IN

10 9 8 7 6 5 4 3 2 1

To Stephanie,
my beautiful wife and the mother of our five children

CONTENTS

CONTENTS

CONTENTS

CONTENTS

ACKNOWLEDGMENTS

I thank all those who made this book possible. My dear wife's sincere support is greatly appreciated, and her beautiful smile brightens my every day. I am grateful to have been raised in such a wonderful family. To my parents, brothers, and sister—I love you all. I greatly value those at Deseret Book, all of whom have continually entrusted me with their confidence, especially my friend Jana Erickson. Finally, I give credit and thanks to those who are represented in this book through their stories. Their faithful examples bless the lives of others and strengthen the Lord's kingdom on earth.

INTRODUCTION

It is an incredible privilege to work on a project associated with the holy temple, whether the project involves a work of art or gathering research about a temple's history from one of the hundreds of amazing people who have played roles in building and maintaining temples around the world. The stories collected in this volume are a result of the latter.

I have worked to represent as many temples, cultures, and themes as possible. And though the Church spans continents, tongues, and political climates, these stories demonstrate that the language of the temple is the same no matter the place. Likewise, the promises of the temple are universal, sought after like precious pearls of great price by all of Heavenly Father's faithful children.

I have given my best effort to record these interviews accurately and reverently. It is said that a journalist is only as accurate as his sources. Believing this to be true, I have, whenever possible, made an exhaustive effort to find multiple credible sources for each story and to be true to a strict standard of conveying the facts without aggrandizement. None of the material in this book was used without expressed permission or without being previously published. On many occasions, spiritually sensitive and personal thoughts were shared and it became inappropriate to continue recording portions of the interview. These moments, recorded only in my heart and memory, will be perhaps the sweetest memories of creating this book.

In every interview, the subject of the temple, combined with the faithfulness of those with whom I was speaking, always fostered feelings of the Spirit—even in the most unlikely of places. I will never forget gathering information for The Hague Netherlands Temple. I met Temple President Anne Hulleman for an interview late in the day. He asked me if I would like to go out to dinner with him and his wife. I agreed. As we drove through the rain, I wondered what kind of native cuisine I would soon be ordering. I stopped wondering when we pulled into the parking lot of a Chinese restaurant. In between wontons and egg rolls we discussed the many wonderful aspects of the temple's history and symbolism. I will never forget thinking, "Here I am: an American in Holland, with the Dutch temple president and matron, eating Chinese food."

The people you meet and the miracles of which you read in this book, combined with any level of desire or hope to have faith, will strengthen your love for the holy temple. I learned a great lesson from a brother who lived in the Edmonton Alberta Temple district. At the temple's open house in 1999, I asked him what the new temple meant to him. He responded with enthusiasm about his and his wife's temple-attendance goals. He explained that for years they could attend the temple in Cardston only once a month because travel time was twelve hours each way. He said, "With a temple so close to home in Edmonton we can now attend the temple once a week because it is *only* six hours to and from the temple." His comments were sincere and full of gratitude. He was grateful for the blessing of having a temple six hours away and yet "so close to home." When I returned home from that trip, I shared the experience with my wife. Now, every time we think of this brother's faithful example, we recommit ourselves to attending the temple as frequently as our personal circumstances allow.

Increased temple attendance is its own small miracle. Indeed, I have found that miracles are synonymous with every aspect of temple work; there is more divine intervention involved in this work than we realize. While serving as project superintendent of the Houston Texas Temple, Brother Leon Rowley made the following observation: "Small or great in our estimation, seen or concealed from view, it seems that miracles do take place in connection with the building of every temple. Some miracles are celebrated with immediate amazement and joy, while others may appear to be trivial matters that we foolishly attribute to coincidence."[1] I believe the more we immerse ourselves in this great work, the more we will be sensitive to the Lord's involvement.

I am hopeful that this collection of sacred events and testimonies will kindle a desire within you to seek for memorable temple experiences in your own life. The experiences I had through gathering these stories have strengthened my own conviction of the truthfulness of the gospel and knowledge that the work of the temple is the greatest work on the face of the earth.

HOLINESS TO THE LORD
THE HOUSE OF THE LORD

BILLINGS MONTANA TE
THE CHURCH OF JESUS CHRIST OF LATTER-DAY
3100 RIM POINT DRIVE

MUSIC STANDS AND SNOW SHOVELS

Billings Montana Temple

A hearty storm blew in for the March 1998 groundbreaking of the Billings Montana Temple, taking Church members and guest dignitaries by surprise. The 4,800 people—from twelve states and two Canadian provinces—in attendance braved freezing temperatures, fog, and snow to be there for the occasion. Teeth chattered as a seven-hundred-member youth choir sang "Now Let Us Rejoice." The spring snowstorm had caught the majority of attendees off guard; and lacking a sufficient number of snow shovels, many used inverted music stands to push away the snow and ice.

The weather worsened at the passing of each hour. One loyal sister in her sixties had arrived two hours early to ensure she would have a front-row seat. Swathed in a blanket under an umbrella, she sat on a lawn chair for more than four hours. When she rose, the perfectly dry ground beneath her chair was ringed by snow five inches deep!

One young man displayed an optimistic attitude, remarking that "the Lord blessed this groundbreaking today with snow to make this temple ground white and pure."[1] Later, Church members learned that the spring snowstorm was a blessing indeed. A large anti-Mormon organization from northern Wyoming had planned to disrupt the groundbreaking proceeding. Not one protester was able to reach the temple site because of the hazardous weather and travel conditions.[2]

THEY NAMED HIM TEMPLE

Aba Nigeria Temple

From the moment the Aba Nigeria Temple was announced in April 2000, members of the Church in that region looked forward to the day they could visit the house of the Lord in their country. Anticipation of the temple's completion grew faster than did the actual walls of the beautiful edifice. When open house dates were announced nearly five years later, members from around western Africa began making plans to visit the temple. Evelyn Momoh and her husband, Wahab, were among those who had longed for years to visit the temple. She and her husband made a four-hour journey on a crowded bus of members to serve as volunteers at the temple open house. Sister Momoh was expecting a baby at the time, and she knew when they made the plans that her due date was near. They took the trip nonetheless, and as their 150-mile journey came to an end, she began having labor pains.

With encouragement from Brother Momoh, the bus driver hurried to the temple complex. Sister Momoh's water broke before arriving, and a volunteer medical team at the temple was ready to assist with the delivery as soon as the Momohs arrived. Born in the temple's parking lot, the Momohs' second son was named Temple.

Meridian Magazine recounted Wahab Momoh's joy at having arrived in time to have the baby born on the temple complex: "I am so excited to have this child born here on this holy spot that I can hardly contain myself," Brother Momoh said. Sister Momoh, who was happy but exhausted, said only, "Thanks be to God we made it. I am so happy!" Mother and baby stayed with a local member to recover from the delivery and gain strength for the trip home.[1]

On the first day the newly dedicated temple was open, Brother and Sister Momoh returned to receive the endowment and to be sealed as a family. As Brother and Sister Momoh participated in temple ceremonies for themselves, members in the waiting room lovingly took care of sleeping baby Temple and his two-year-old brother. The family was among the first to be sealed in the Aba Nigeria Temple.[2]

The Salt Lake Temple was dedicated during thirty-one sessions between April 6 and April 24, 1893, by President Wilford Woodruff. Late in the evening, at the conclusion of a dedicatory session on April 7, Emma Bennett of Provo, Utah, gave birth to a son within the walls of the temple. James E. Talmage recorded the facts about the experience in his diary, writing: "A Sister Bennett from Provo was taken with labor pains and gave easy birth to a son. She was removed from the Assembly Room to a small apartment [in the temple]. Some sects would hold that such an event desecrated the holy place; but the Latter-day Saints will take a directly opposite view."[3]

Eight days later, parents Benjamin and Emma Bennett returned to the temple for the newborn to receive a blessing by Joseph F. Smith. In the blessing the baby boy was named Joseph Temple Bennett.[4]

SECURITY WATCHDOG

Washington D. C. Temple

During construction of the Washington D.C. Temple in early 1973, leaders became concerned with security at the temple site. On a Saturday about this time a stray German shepherd appeared near the temple gates. Residents in the area called animal control to pick up the dog, but when work began the next Monday morning, the dog was still there. Taking pity on the hungry dog, workers fed him and decided to keep him on the site. Zacharias, as the workers called him, soon became an important part of the temple construction site's security. After sleeping during the day, the dog regularly woke at 4 P.M. to watch the workers depart. Then the dog made rounds on the property throughout the night. On one occasion, Zacharias led a security man to the temple president's office, where a fire was burning, apparently caused by a mishap with welding equipment. When the temple was completed, one of the workers took the trusted dog home with him. The construction foreman said they believed that the faithful German shepherd was sent by the Lord to help meet security needs at the temple site.[1]

On the east and west ends of the Washington D.C. Temple are seven-foot-wide, W-shaped windows that run from the ground all the way to the top of the temple. The glass near the ground is colored in rich, vibrant reds and oranges. As the windows rise, the colors become progressively lighter of blues, violets, and finally white. This succession of colors suggests the way the temple can shift visitors' minds from earthly concerns to thoughts of eternity. The windows rise unbroken to the top of the building, symbolizing the possibility of man's eternal growth.[2]

TEMPLE SPARED DURING MILITARY CONFLICT

Manila Philippines Temple

In December 1989, combat associated with a military coup in the Philippines came dangerously close to destroying the Manila Philippines Temple. As the coup erupted, heavy fighting took place at Camp Aguinaldo, a military base neighboring the temple grounds. The small Filipino staff still inside the temple complex at the time could hear confusion closing in as rebel troops attacked the government loyalists at Camp Aguinaldo, dropping bombs and firing rockets. On the second day of fighting, rebel soldiers breached the temple gates and occupied the grounds. Members throughout the Philippines prayed that the temple might somehow be spared.

By late the next evening, government troops had the upper hand in the battle, but the temple annex and grounds—the last remaining rebel stronghold in Manila—were still in enemy hands. A government commander gave the rebels one hour to surrender and announced plans to attack with heavy artillery at 11:00 P.M. if his ultimatum was not met. The grim circumstance was reported to Elder Dallin H. Oaks, of the Quorum of the Twelve Apostles, thirty minutes before the 11:00 P.M. deadline. It was then 7:30 A.M. Sunday in Salt Lake City. Elder Oaks described the events that immediately transpired:

"By a remarkable coincidence—one of those happenings that cannot be coincidental—the First Presidency and Quorum of the Twelve Apostles had scheduled an unusual meeting that Sunday morning. At 8:00 A.M., 3 December, just 30 minutes after I received that alarming report from Manila, the assembled First Presidency and Quorum of the Twelve bowed in prayer and pleaded with the Lord to intervene to protect His house. Elder Marvin J. Ashton led our prayer. As we prayed, it was 11:00 P.M. Sunday evening in Manila, the exact hour appointed for the assault.

"The attack never came. Twenty minutes after our prayer [Area] President [George I.] Cannon phoned Church headquarters to report that the military commander had unexpectedly decided against a night assault. Early the next morning [I received word] that the rebels had melted away during the night. I recorded in my journal, 'I consider this a miracle of divine intervention no less impressive than many recorded in holy writ.'"[1]

A MORMON PILGRIMAGE
Freiberg Germany Temple

On November 23, 1992, a group of Ukrainian Saints left Kiev on an historic journey to the Freiberg Germany Temple. President Howard L. Biddulph, who was presiding over the Ukraine Kiev Mission at the time, recorded: "For the first time, a group of Ukrainian Latter-day Saints would cross what had been an impenetrable western frontier of the former Soviet Union to undertake what government authorities called 'the Mormon pilgrimage.'"[1] For most in the group of twenty-two men, women, and children, this was the first trip outside the borders of the former Soviet Union.

After months of red tape to secure necessary approvals, the group traveled by bus thousands of miles through the nations of the former Communist Bloc. The expense was enormous—the equivalent of a year's tithing for most who made the trip. Ukrainian currency could not be converted, so the travelers had to carry with them their own food, sleeping bags, and other provisions sufficient for the trip. Realizing that most would not have any available funds for shopping or sightseeing in the West, all of the travelers agreed that it would be better if none of them were to do so. Instead, they planned to devote every available moment to temple work.

To pass the time on their lengthy bus journey, the members sang hymns, shared testimonies, and read scriptures. When they at last arrived in Freiberg they could not find the temple due to low-lying fog. As anticipation mounted, the temple's spire finally appeared, beautifully lit above the foggy haze. All on board cried out with great joy and thanksgiving. Next to the temple was the first LDS meetinghouse any of them had ever seen, where they were greeted by loving German temple workers.

The next day, in the house of the Lord, the Ukrainian couples and families were sealed for eternity. President Biddulph described the events of the trip in his book, *The Morning Breaks*, writing: "The adults were endowed, and couples were sealed for eternity. Then those who had brought children with them were sealed as eternal families. Each adult then performed two endowment sessions for the dead . . . and three [the next day]. . . .

"Gradually, through two, full, wonderful days in the house of the Lord, their comprehension of his glorious promises grew significantly. Sacred spiritual experiences were enjoyed by some, and all were edified in various ways. . . .

"One of the leaders described his experience in two sentences: 'Until we experience and understand the temple, we are but schoolchildren in the gospel of Jesus Christ. The temple is the higher spiritual university of the gospel and Church of Jesus Christ.'"[2]

Smiles, acts of kindness, and the unified love of the gospel overcame language barriers between temple patrons and workers. German Saints demonstrated Christlike charity by preparing meals for the visitors and even gave gifts and money to their new friends. Although the gifts were graciously accepted, the recipients agreed that the money should go to a fund for future Ukrainian pilgrimages. The Saints' long return trip was one of great optimism and rejoicing in the blessings of the temple.

This initial pilgrimage had a wonderful, widespread effect on the Church in the Ukraine and other parts of the former Soviet Union. Trips to Freiberg dramatically increased, and over the next two years, more than two hundred Latter-day Saints from Kiev received their temple blessings. President Biddulph wrote that "many families of very modest means have borne witness that their sacrifices have been attended by a miraculous opening of the 'the windows of heaven' to bless them with means sufficient to attend the temple. Freiberg temple workers have described the special spirit that Latter-day Saints from Ukraine, Belarus, and Russia bring into the temple. They are touched . . . by the great piety and reverence of these Latter-day Saints from the East. They have witnessed them pray fervently together before entering the temple and reverently touch or embrace the outside masonry of the temple as a final act of loving farewell."[3]

DISCOVERING THE NAUVOO TEMPLE BLUEPRINTS

Nauvoo Illinois Temple

Sister Marjorie Hopkins Bennion learned a remarkable story about the Nauvoo Temple blueprints when she met Sandra Griffin Hardy, a great-great-granddaughter of William Weeks, the Nauvoo Temple architect. Sister Bennion said:

"In 1948, a young missionary from Heber City, Utah, Elder Vern C. Thacker, was transferred to the small, remote town of Boron, California, in the Mojave Desert. While there he and his companion, Elder Frank Gifford, knocked on the door of the home of Mr. and Mrs. Leslie M. Griffin, who graciously greeted them. Mr. Griffin was not a member of the Church but told the missionaries he was a grandson of William Weeks, the architect of the 'old Mormon temple in Nauvoo, Illinois.' Although Leslie remembered little of his grandfather, he knew William was very proud of his role as [temple] architect. . . . The two Mormon missionaries developed a good relationship with the Griffin family. . . . Before Thacker was to return home to Utah following the completion of his mission, Griffin turned the temple drawings over to him with instructions for him to deliver them to Church headquarters in Salt Lake City. Thacker recalled the scene:

"'On our last visit to Mr. Griffin he excused himself for a few minutes and went into the rear part of his house. He returned with a large roll of papers about three feet long, ten inches in diameter, secured with a rubber band. He explained, 'These are the original architect's drawings for the Nauvoo Temple. They have been in my

family for 100 years, handed down from my grandfather, William Weeks." He opened the bundle. . . . There were exterior drawings, some interior, an angel on a weather vane, pencil sketches for circular stairways, circular windows, archways, etc. Even the measurements for various details of the temple were included in William's handwriting. They were yellowed with age but in amazingly good condition. Mr. Griffin knew I was returning home in a few days. He asked me if I would do him a favor of carrying these plans to the [Church's] headquarters. I assured him that it would be a great honor for me to do so. He said he felt strongly that, after 100 years, these should be given to the Church. I subsequently left Boron with the plans tucked into the turtle back trunk of my Ford.'

"One week after returning from his mission, Thacker made an appointment with [Church historian] A. William Lund . . . and turned the drawings over to him. A short time later, Griffin received a letter of thanks from Lund. . . . 'We appreciate your action far more than words can express.'"[1]

On Easter Sunday, April 4, 1999, during general conference, President Gordon B. Hinckley made the historic announcement that the Nauvoo Temple would be rebuilt. During his closing remarks, President Hinckley stated, "I feel impressed to announce that among all of the temples we are constructing, we plan to rebuild the Nauvoo Temple. . . . The new building will stand as a memorial to those who built the first such structure there on the banks of the Mississippi."[2] The architect's drawings recovered by Elders Thacker and Gifford were key instruments in making possible the accurate rebuilding of the Nauvoo Temple.

The modern Nauvoo Illinois Temple is fifteen feet shorter than the original Nauvoo Temple. The modern temple has six floors and is topped with a vertical angel Moroni statue. The original temple featured a horizontal, gilded angel with a trumpet. According to Thomas L. Kane, the angel was added to the temple's spire by the Saints who stayed behind in Nauvoo to finish the temple.[3] It is said that the original angel represented the angel in John's vision in the New Testament book of Revelation: "And I saw another angel fly in the midst of heaven, having the everlasting gospel to preach unto them that dwell on the earth" (Revelation 14:6).

THE HOUSE WAS GUARDED

Kirtland Temple

As a father, missionary, and architect, Truman O. Angell made a great contribution to building the kingdom during the earliest years of the restored gospel. At the age of seventy-four, he recorded in his journal a meaningful experience he had witnessed years earlier while at the Kirtland Temple:

"After the building was dedicated, a few of us, some six or eight, having Patriarch Joseph Smith, Sr., in company, went morning and evening to pray, entering at the west end of the [Kirtland] Temple and going clear through to the east stand. This we enjoyed very much. The stand being enclosed by curtains or veils made it quite by itself and a good place to pray with none to molest. One evening, having been in the country, I was too late to enter with the brethren. The company would not emerge till quite dark. I had tried the door and knew they were at prayer. I felt out of place and went to my house, but soon came out and met Brother Brigham Young, inquiring for Oliver Cowdery. I said I had not seen him.

"We walked out towards the [Kirtland] Temple, approaching the building on the side which was used for the Prophet Joseph and his counselors, a portion of the attic on the east being especially appropriated to their use. In the said attic, and right over the stand where the brethren were praying in the hall below, were two windows in the gable end to help give light to his compartment or

room, the windows being 12 or 14 feet apart, and unusually high from the floor; being nearly 4 feet to the bottom of the lower sash.

"When about ten rods distant we looked up and saw two personages, before each window, leaving and approaching each other like guards would do. This continued until quite dark. As they were walking back and forth, one turned his face to me for an instant; but while they walked to and fro, only a side view was visible. I have no doubt that the house was guarded, as I have had no other way to account for it. I insert this note thinking it may do someone good as it has me."[1]

A SPECIAL SESSION

London England Temple

For decades, the London England and Bern Switzerland Temples were the only temples on the European continent. They served a large geographical area that included districts on the African continent. Many members made tremendous sacrifices to attend these temples, knowing that a temple trip could be a once-in-a-lifetime event.

In the late 1980s, a couple from Ghana in western Africa saved their money and traveled to the London Temple on an uncomfortable freight vessel. They arrived in England on a Friday night and awoke the next morning eager to visit the temple. With the help of a deckhand from the freighter, they found the temple Saturday afternoon. Their anticipation turned to sorrow when they learned that the temple was closed on Saturday afternoons; the last session of the day had begun a half hour before their arrival. The temple would reopen the following Tuesday—the same time their freighter would be returning to Ghana.

After traveling a vast distance at great cost, the couple was overwhelmed with anguish and feared their dreams of achieving temple blessings would not be realized. They broke into tears. Arthur Henry King, who served as president of the London England Temple from 1986 to 1990, soon learned of the couple's plight. President King arranged for a few temple workers and local members to participate in a special, additional session that day. His actions allowed this

humble African couple to receive their endowments and the sealing ordinance that afternoon. They left the temple late in the day filled with the peace and joy found in temple blessings.[1]

The site of the London England Temple is rich in tradition and historic lore. The first known mention of the property is in the Doomsday Book, a record of a survey of the lands of England by order of William the Conqueror around 1086. In 1953, the property was purchased by the Church. For a time, the Church rented a portion of the property as a horse pasture to Sir Winston Churchill when he purchased an adjoining estate and became a neighbor.

A TRAIL OF TEARS TO THE TEMPLE

Dallas Texas and Logan Utah Temples

In the winter of 1831, thousands of Native Americans from the Choctaw Nation walked what became known as the Trail of Tears. Their destination was Oklahoma, where they were being exiled by the United States government. It was a frigid winter and provisions were scarce. Hundreds died and were buried along the trail.

One hundred fifty-two years later, on September 11, 1983, Linda A. Stokes of Logan, Utah, woke in the early morning after an amazing dream.

"I [had] learned," Sister Stokes wrote, "that my Choctaw great-great-great-grandmother, Betsy Perkins, had left Mississippi with the tribe and had walked the 'Trail of Tears' to Oklahoma. I placed her name in my family records, but I thought that I could do nothing further on that line. As far as I knew, no further information was available."

Her dream changed everything. "I dreamed that I saw a native American woman with long braids streaked with gray. She was stirring something in a cooking pot. In my dream, I was in her home. . . . The woman spoke with me, and we conversed for some time. I was at ease in her presence and felt her warm hospitality. I don't remember what was said, but she told me her name over and over again—*Nanah-ku-chi*. Another woman was with her, holding a child about two or three years old. They were all dressed in what appeared to be buckskin—it was chamois-colored and simple in design."[1]

Following a prompting from the Spirit, Sister Stokes got out of bed and recorded her experience. "The Spirit made known to me," she explained, "that, if I were faithful, I would be led to find my ancestors' names, and that *Nanah-ku-chi*, one of the women I had seen in the dream, was my ancestor. I seemed to hear in my mind, 'Now is the time to labor for thy dead.'"[2]

After returning to her bed, Sister Stokes was soon awakened by her three-year-old son, who exclaimed, "Indians, Indians, I dreamed about Indians." Her son explained that the Indian in his dream was a chief and had asked the young boy for some bread. The boy had taken the chief to the kitchen, but was told: "No, not that kind of bread."[3]

These dreams sent Sister Stokes on a personal crusade to gather as much information as possible about her Choctaw ancestors. Her journeys took her to the National Archives in Washington, D.C.; the Family History Library in Salt Lake City; Philadelphia, Mississippi; and Oklahoma. She wrote, "I asked a Choctaw from Oklahoma if he knew the meaning of the word *Nanah-ku-chi*. He told me that it means 'to bring out of the mountain.' . . . I concluded that the words I had heard must have meant that the names of the Choctaw dead should be brought out of obscurity so that the Choctaws' temple work should be completed."[4]

When her research was completed, 1,500 names from the record were sent to the Dallas Texas Temple and another 1,500 names were sent to the Logan Utah Temple, where Sister Stokes and many others performed temple work for the Choctaw people.

Of this great labor of love, Sister Stokes bore testimony that "though [the Choctaws] had once walked the 'Trail of Tears,' now they could walk the straight and narrow path of joy that leads to eternal life."[5]

REMEMBER THE ALAMO

Dallas Texas Temple

The phrase "Remember the Alamo!" took on a spiritual meaning for three months in 1986 at the Dallas Texas Temple. Inspired by President Gordon B. Hinckley's comments at one of the temple's dedicatory sessions, several Texas Saints began an exhaustive, two-year effort to gather data for those who had defended the Alamo on March 6, 1836.

After years of research, temple ordinances were performed for those patriotic men who had fought and died at the Alamo. Four hundred twenty-five individuals received temple blessings between October and December 1986. Of those names, 183 were defenders of the Alamo; the rest were spouses and children of those men. Youth in the temple district performed the baptisms, and other temple patrons performed the remaining ordinances. The final ordinances were performed on the last day the temple was open that year—the same year the Texas Sesquicentennial recognized the Alamo defense.[1]

LEARNING FROM MISTAKES

Denver Colorado Temple

The Church faced intense public opposition while selecting a site for the Denver Colorado Temple. When the first proposed site was publicly announced, nearby residents immediately launched a campaign to stop the "Mormon Project." The *Denver Post* ran a front-page story describing residents as "disturbed, infuriated and angry" about the Church's proposal to build a temple in their community. One resident was quoted as saying: "The community is in a state of shock and panic. We can't imagine investing 15 years in this community, developing the land, keeping open space, protecting the view and have an abomination like this coming. It's absolutely frightening."[1] Within weeks, plans were made to search for another site for the temple.

The second proposed site also received bitter opposition. This time, a committee of citizens in Cherry Hills Village worked to block city approval of the temple because it would have six spires and thus violate city zoning laws. The Church worked simultaneously to receive a variance from the city's code. During the citizens' protest, rumors circulated through the community, including: "The building will be as big as the Salt Lake Temple"; "Mormons are a cult; they'll be brainwashing Cherry Creek West students across the street"; and "Property values will plummet."[2] In a variety of forums, Church leaders painstakingly answered community questions, trying to resolve concerns and clear up

misconceptions. The opposition remained firm; and disappointed but not discouraged, Church leaders made plans to search for another temple site.

In a matter of only four months, two sites had been rejected. The temple's design—a six-spire building similar to the Boise temple—had proved a major deterrent in gaining approval for the project. Over the next few months, the search committee reviewed a final site and discussed changing architectural plans to resemble the design of the Atlanta Georgia Temple. These architectural changes proved to be a valuable selling point when trying to win over government officials and residents near the third site. This third and eventually providential site was a hilltop that had once featured a nine-hole golf course and country club. Joseph H. Barton, a local land developer and member of the Denver Temple committee, described his first impressions of the place: "I'd never set foot on the land until that time, but as I stood for the first time on the spot where the club house used to be—and where the temple is now—I was awed by the gorgeous unobstructed view. I had the strongest feeling that this was the right site."[3]

After receiving approval to begin construction, Barton recorded: "We didn't realize the forces Satan can muster when he really puts his mind to stopping a project. . . . Literally all hell broke loose when we announced the first two sites to the public. We weren't welcome at those locations. After much prayer and consideration, we realized as a committee that we just hadn't done our homework. We needed much more preparation to achieve success, so over the next six months we really went to work and did the job right. Our intensive planning and preparation paid off. We obtained the third site—the right site—with very little opposition. Had we gone ahead with the site we're at now without knowing what kind of blockades Satan was setting up for us, we would have failed. I bear testimony we have the right site and the Lord helped us to get it by diverting our attention elsewhere until we learned the proper procedures to get approval. Had we initially proceeded with [the third] site, in our ignorance we would have spoiled the Lord's choice. He didn't let us do that. He works through us [but] we had to do our homework. I am now convinced the Lord allowed us to practice on the wrong sites."[4]

All of the altars in the Denver Colorado Temple are covered with delicate, handmade lace created by sisters in the temple district. Tatting, the art of making lace by looping and knotting a single strand of fine thread on a small hand shuttle, is time consuming and tedious work. Each of the nineteen sisters who participated in this labor of love spent hundreds of hours tatting a cloth. One sister related: "It was very detailed work and mistakes were inevitable. I couldn't untie those countless tiny knots to make them right. The only way to correct the mistakes was to cut them out. Sometimes I wouldn't discover the mistakes right away and I had to clip out hours of work.

"That's just like life. We make mistakes but through repentance we can cut out those parts of our lives. If we catch them early it isn't quite so painful, but it's never too late to excise even the biggest one."[5]

ROLLING IN SNOW

Freiberg Germany Temple

In the years following the announcement and construction of the Freiberg Germany Temple, Elder Thomas S. Monson was often asked how the Church could obtain permission to build a temple behind the Iron Curtain. President Thomas S. Monson answered: "My feeling is simply that the faith and devotion of Latter-day Saints in that area brought forth the help of Almighty God and provided for them the eternal blessings which they so richly deserve."[1]

A few months after the temple was dedicated, Henry Burkhardt, president of the Freiberg Germany Temple, discovered early one morning that baptisms had not been performed for 108 males scheduled for that day. He felt that the work should go on even though the heat was off and the water in the font was icy cold. He called Andreas Kleinert, a faithful teenager who lived nearby, and thirty minutes later they entered the freezing water. "When I immersed for the first time, it felt like I was rolling in snow," said Andreas. "I just could not get used to the cold water." Still, they determined to go on until the 108 baptisms had been finished. Andreas commented, "Never had I shivered like this before. But neither President Burkhardt nor I even caught a cold. I was happy that I was once again able to do work in the temple."[2]

SPIRE BURNT TO A CINDER

Hermosillo Sonora Mexico Temple

In July 1999, the spire of the Hermosillo Sonora Mexico Temple was carefully placed atop the newly constructed temple. One day, a number of construction workers were on the roof doing work when a severe and quickly moving thunderstorm approached. The workers were hurriedly trying to get off the roof when a lightning bolt hit the spire on the neighboring meetinghouse and burnt it to a cinder. Some of the men were in such close proximity to the flash of lightning that they were forced off their feet and stunned by the powerful explosion of electric power. Herardo Rivera, the temple's historian, felt that the event was indeed remarkable: "The height of the temple's metal spire resting on the temple reached sixty-nine feet. The neighboring chapel's spire has a metal spire that reached only twenty feet."[1] News of this wondrous event spread rapidly through the temple district. For generations, members will be able to view the graceful temple spire and remember that by divine intervention lives were spared.

The Hermosillo Sonora Mexico Temple celebrated its groundbreaking in December 1998. The members were so enthusiastic about having a temple that they began beautifying the unattractive boulevard that ran along the front of the temple. Professional landscape plans were created and then implemented by the members, who anxiously volunteered their labor. Clutter was cleared away, ground was made level, fertile soil was brought in, and inviting gardens were planted. Herardo Rivera, Hermosillo Sonora Mexico Temple historian said, "We would work in the evenings and at night, whenever we could, and we left the spot very precious and beautiful. . . . It has given us great joy to know that we have participated in something that has to do with the temple."[2]

THE LORD SELECTS A TEMPLE SITE

Houston Texas Temple

Selecting a location for the house of the Lord requires patience, determination and, often, a miracle or two. Site selection for the Houston Texas Temple was no different. By spring 1997, after an extensive evaluation process, six qualifying properties were being considered. Steven R. Cook, a Houston realtor and Church member, hosted Ted Simmons, head of the Church's real estate department, on a tour of the six properties. During the tour, Brother Simmons was drawn to a lovely location *across the street* from one of the six selected sites. This spot was located on Champion Forest Drive and stood on a twenty-acre parcel of land with tall mature trees.

The prime acreage was owned by Don Hand, a successful Houston developer. When Brother Cook called to express interest in purchasing the property, Mr. Hand made his position clear with the response: "There's no amount of money that would interest me in selling that property." The Church was just one of many who had expressed interest in the site, and he had refused them all. Mr. Hand considered that location to be the "crown jewel" of all his properties.

On June 6, 1997, President Gordon B. Hinckley arrived to visit all the potential temple sites. The Champion Forest Drive location was not officially available, but Brother Simmons introduced it to President Hinckley nonetheless.

HOUSTON TEXAS TEMPLE
THE CHURCH OF JESUS CHRIST OF LATTER-DAY SAINTS

Just a few weeks later, President Hinckley had made his decision. He notified Brother Simmons that the temple would be built on Champion Forest Drive—the location Don Hand would not sell for "any amount of money." Both Brother Simmons and Brother Cook wondered how they might acquire a property when its owner had no intention of selling.

But the Lord knows where and how His temples will be built. Within fifteen minutes of learning about President Hinckley's decision, Brother Cook received a phone call. It was Don Hand, requesting a meeting with Brother Cook as soon as possible.

At the meeting, Mr. Hand told Brother Cook of the terrible weekend he had had as he contemplated whether to sell his property to the Church. Don and his wife, Judy, had reviewed some of the material Brother Cook had prepared about the temple and had spent the weekend pacing the floors as they thought about the possibility of selling. After a sleepless weekend, he and his wife had decided to sell the land to the Church for what he called the "Mormon cathedral."

Don explained that earlier life events had influenced his decision to sell to the Church. He told Brother Cook about a time in the 1980s when the struggling Houston real estate market resulted in the Hands losing almost all their assets. While in the depths of financial despair, Don had prayed and asked for the Lord's help, promising that he would "make it right" if the Lord blessed him. Don soon recognized the divine intervention that helped his business recover and flourish. Wanting to keep his promise, Don had given a substantial anonymous donation to his own church, but he still felt that he should do more. He and his wife felt that selling the property to the Church was the right thing to do; indeed, it would be the "crown jewel" of his property if the temple were located there.

Brother Cook later said, "My meeting with Don Hand was almost like a testimony meeting as he expressed his love for the Lord and his desire to become 'one with the Lord.' The same spirit that inspired President Hinckley had inspired Mr. Hand, and on exactly the same weekend."[1]

When the Church purchased the property for the Houston Texas Temple from Don Hand, it gave the seller the right to approve the final architectural design. The first design proposed to Mr. Hand was a design similar to the Billings Montana Temple. He felt the one-story design did not suit the area. The final design was patterned after the majestic Washington D.C. chapel, the first LDS chapel built east of the Rocky Mountains after the Saints' exodus west. This chapel—though no longer owned by the Church—is now a national landmark, located only a short distance from the White House.

MANY WAYS TO CONTRIBUTE

Jordan River Utah Temple

The Jordan River Temple is situated on a fifteen-acre site atop a slight hill, making it clearly visible from many parts of the Salt Lake Valley. Unlike some of the other temples, the Jordan River Temple was funded entirely by contributions from members living in the area. In 1978, a large fund-raising campaign was begun in all 122 stakes from the Salt Lake and Jordan River Utah Temple districts. When the campaign ended just over a year later, the members had contributed $14.5 million—110 percent of the original goal.

This vast amount of money came from the sacrifices of thousands of members for their new temple. David L. McKay and Mildred C. McKay, of the Murray Utah Stake, collected dozens of stories about the sacrifice and hard work contributed by members during this fund-raising campaign. What follows is a sampling of those stories.

"A woman with cataracts to the point that she [could not] see eight inches from her face had been saving to have an operation to restore her sight. She took the entire savings that she had accumulated for this operation, emptied the entire account, and gave everything for the temple."[1]

One woman in the temple district had been struggling with many problems, including smoking. Accompanied by her daughter, she told her bishop in an interview that although she didn't have much she could contribute to the temple

fund, she would donate as much as she was spending on her cigarettes. The bishop encouraged the sister in this idea but asked her to promise that she would *first* give up her habit of smoking and then give the money she would have spent on cigarettes to the temple fund. In that setting she found the courage to promise that she would quit. With great enthusiasm the three knelt in prayer to thank the Lord for His inspiration and help in this sister's life.[2]

Two young brothers, ages eight and ten, were excited to do their part in raising money for the temple. The two walked from door to door down the street, asking their neighbors if they would like to buy homemade bread. Before long they had requests for sixteen loaves. They hurried home and told their unsuspecting mother that they needed her to bake sixteen loaves of bread right away. Their mother agreed to join in this fund-raising venture, and before long, sixteen hot loaves of bread were delivered. In all, the team sold about thirty loaves for the temple fund.[3]

One man put aside one dollar a day for the temple for the duration of the fund-raising campaign. To do this, the man, who made less than a hundred dollars a week to support his wife and three children, went without lunch every day of the year-long campaign.

One member did not have an immediate desire to contribute to the new temple. She initially believed it was not fair to expect the members to pay for their temple entirely on their own. Her attitude softened as she shared her thoughts with a co-worker one day. She said, "I don't see why the members are expected to do it all by themselves. I think it ought to be 50-50." Her co-worker responded, "Have you stopped to think that in countries of South America, people who don't have anything but little homes with dirt floors are sacrificing and actually giving the gold out of their teeth [to pay for temples]?" The sister explained, "It made me stop and think. The more I thought about it the more I realized that you only appreciate fully the things you have to sacrifice for. . . . It made me realize that [contributing to the temple] is not an obligation but a privilege."[4]

FUTURE TEMPLE SEEN IN A DREAM
Kona Hawaii Temple

The Kona Hawaii Temple is a blessing for the Saints on the big island of Hawaii. Due to the inspired leadership of Kona Stake President Philip Harris, the Saints of Kona were being prepared for the temple years before it was announced. Humbled by the calling to lead the stake, President Harris described how he began his ministry: "When I was first called to be stake president in February of 1997, I wanted to know what the Lord wanted me to accomplish in my term of office. Early in my call, I made it a matter of prayer, pondering, and concern. One night I dreamed I saw a temple in Kona. I woke and told my wife."[1]

At the time, smaller temples were not part of the Church's plans, and President Harris knew that the area over which he presided could not meet the requirements for building a large temple like the one on Oahu. "I therefore interpreted my dream to be a direction for me as a stake president," he said. "I was to make my people temple worthy and temple ready. I based my stake conference talk on the theme of the temple. We were going to become a temple-ready and temple-worthy people."[2]

President Harris put his plan into action by evaluating the long-held tradition of lengthy temple excursions to the Laie Hawaii Temple. After a careful cost analysis, he discovered it was less expensive to make frequent one-day trips to

the temple than less-frequent lengthy temple excursions. The result was an increase in regular and consistent temple attendance.

The spirit and blessings of the temple swelled in the hearts of Saints as they were unknowingly being prepared for a temple closer to home. President Harris held back the tears as he recalled first learning about the Kona Hawaii Temple. He said, "President Hinckley made the announcement of the smaller temples. As I sat in that meeting I wanted to stand and shout because I knew in my lifetime I would see here the temple I had seen in my dream."[3] President Harris was the stake president in Kona when the temple was dedicated in January 2000.

CELESTIAL WINDOWS PROTECTED
DURING EARTHQUAKE

Las Vegas Nevada Temple

In October 1989, a 7.1-magnitude earthquake hit the San Francisco Bay Area just before the third game of the World Series at Candlestick Park. It was the worst earthquake since 1906, collapsing a section of the San Francisco–Oakland Bay Bridge and causing nearly three billion dollars worth of damage in San Francisco alone. Scientists later determined that the quake's epicenter was near Mt. Loma Prieta in Santa Cruz County.

On the day of the quake, the window that was to be hung in the celestial room of the Las Vegas Nevada Temple was in a glass factory in Santa Cruz, hanging in a sling where it was scheduled to be polished and then shipped to the temple. It had taken six weeks to make the window, and the temple's open house was only two weeks away. When the tremor hit, the window swung wildly but amazingly escaped any damage. Other glass projects in the factory were shattered, ruined beyond repair. The window arrived, intact, one week before the temple opened for public viewing.[1]

LAS VEGAS TEMPLE
THE CHURCH OF JESUS CHRIST OF LATTER-DAY SAINTS

A NEWSPAPER FROM ENGLAND

Logan Utah Temple

The day after the Logan Utah Temple was dedicated on May 17, 1884, Bishop Henry Ballard of the Logan Second Ward was busy interviewing members and writing temple recommends when his young daughter Ellen delivered a newspaper to him. The paper was the *Newbury Weekly News*, which was published in his birthplace of Newbury, Berkshire, England. The paper's date—May 15, 1884—indicated that it had been printed only *three* days earlier. At the time, a typical trip across the ocean, and then the plains, took weeks!

Bishop Ballard's young daughter explained that she had been playing on the sidewalk when two strangers handed her the paper and gave strict instructions that she deliver it to no one except her father. Upon inspection, Bishop Ballard found that the newspaper contained a story with the names of sixty people and their accompanying dates of birth and death.

The next day, Bishop Ballard sought an explanation from the temple president, Marriner W. Merrill. After listening to the bishop's story, President Merrill said, "Brother Ballard, someone on the other side is anxious for their work to be done and they knew that you would do it if this paper got into your hands."[1] Bishop Ballard made certain the temple work was complete, and later it was learned that most of the people named in the newspaper were related to the Ballard family.

More than a half-century later, a young M. Russell Ballard, a great-grandson of Henry Ballard, was serving a mission in England and made a visit to the offices of the *Newbury Weekly News.* "I visited the *Newbury Weekly News*," he records, "and verified that the newspaper had never been postdated or mailed out early. I held the issue of 15 May 1884 in my hands and photographed it. There is no mortal way that, in 1884, it could have reached Logan from Newbury within three days."[2]

AND THERE WAS LIGHT

Lubbock Texas Temple

As part of a massive public relations campaign for the Lubbock Texas Temple open house, temple committee chairman Jay B. Jensen was tasked with procuring a photograph of the temple to go on 500,000 newspaper inserts. The photograph would be a vital part of the temple's public unveiling. Immediate publication deadlines required that the photograph be taken regardless of landscape or weather conditions.

Arrangements were promptly made to have a photographer and a rented cherry picker at the temple on a specific day in February. The hoist was to raise the photographer, allowing for an elevated perspective of the temple. Jensen described the morning of the photo shoot in his personal writings as "cold, blustery, cloudy, and dreary. . . .

"The photo shoot was to begin at 4:00 P.M.," he recalled. "The weather and dark gray clouds persisted throughout the day—these would provide a poor background for the gray granite of the temple. I remained at the temple site until 3:00 P.M. when I returned home on a brief errand. As I drove home the clouds were as dense as earlier with no visible blue in the sky. At 3:30 P.M. I returned to the temple site. As I drove west I was looking into a beautiful blue sky punctuated with only scattered fluffy white clouds."[1]

By the time the photographer arrived, the sky and clouds were working together to form a beautiful contrast and backdrop for the shimmering temple. The afternoon sun provided ideal lighting and shadow conditions. The resulting photograph was a wonderful success and provided a memorable image for the cover of the newspaper insert.

Of the day's events, Brother Jensen made this faithful observation: "Skeptics would argue that these events were simply a happy coincidence but I will ever remain convinced otherwise. I believe that blue sky at the right time was the result of divine intervention as Heavenly Father responded to the pleadings of an anxious son. I believe that once again, though with less profound results, He said, 'Let there be Light,' and there was light."[2]

AN ANGEL'S HALO

Newport Beach California Temple

On January 13, 2005, an important milestone in the construction of the Church's 122nd temple was reached. On this day the Newport Beach California Temple was adorned with its golden angel Moroni statue. The chilly morning started out overcast and gloomy. It had rained previously, causing the construction site to be slippery and muddy. Some expressed disappointment that it was not a more bright and sunny day.

Elder Vaughn and Sister Juanee Baird, who were serving as project missionaries, were among the group of about one hundred people gathered to watch the anticipated event. Sister Baird described the proceedings: "The angel was stored in a trailer. Workers carefully uncrated the statue and began to take the bubble wrap off in preparation for it to be lifted by the crane. As they started to unwrap the statue, the sunlight started to shine through the clouds. The sun shining through the mist caused a halo of light to form around the temple spire. As the statue was attached to the crane and slowly hoisted onto the spire, the halo grew bigger and bigger. The bright ring of light perfectly circled the spire and statue the entire time the angel was being installed. It was just incredible!"[1]

Everyone present witnessed the phenomenon in awe. Photographs were taken, including one that was printed the next day in the *Orange County Register,*

whose circulation is larger than that of the *Los Angeles Times*. Although some may consider it to be only an atmospheric wonder, many members and Church leaders considered it to be a sign of divine acceptance.

DODGING A HURRICANE

Raleigh North Carolina Temple

On September 15, 1999, Mother Nature poised herself to deliver a powerful punch to the East Coast of the United States. The storm came in the form of Floyd, a category-four hurricane that prompted millions of people to evacuate a long stretch of coastline. The massive storm was headed directly toward the Carolina coast but weakened before making landfall in the wee hours of September 16. Even so, Floyd was blamed for more than forty deaths and perhaps $1 billion in losses, much due to flooding. Trees that had withstood the elements for decades were left barely standing in waterlogged soil, and then toppled over like bowling pins. An astonishing path of destruction lay in the storm's wake.

Miraculously, the only sign of Floyd at the Raleigh North Carolina Temple—which was directly in the hurricane's path before it changed direction—were puddles of water on the construction site.[1]

The Salt Lake Temple is 253,000 square feet. The Raleigh North Carolina Temple is 10,700 square feet—about 1/25th the size of the Salt Lake Temple.

The Raleigh North Carolina Temple set a record for the fastest completion of a temple. The temple required about 200 days to build, 40 days fewer than the average for similar smaller temples.

OPEN THE BLIND EYES

Houston Texas Temple

In Isaiah the Lord said, "Behold my servant, whom I uphold; mine elect, in whom my soul delighteth; I have put my spirit upon him. . . . I the Lord have called thee in righteousness, and will hold thine hand, and will keep thee, and give thee for a covenant of the people, for a light of the Gentiles; to open the blind eyes" (Isaiah 42:1, 6–7). For Elder Terry and Sister Shirley Holmes, called as Houston Texas Temple construction missionaries, these were prophetic words.

Nearly four years before his call, Brother Holmes had a near-fatal heart attack. A miraculous recovery suggested to him that the Lord still had a work for him to perform. He thus accepted his call with honor, knowing how important his responsibilities would be. Still, he was concerned about his heart problems and his eyesight that was progressively worsening.

Project manager Leon Rowley recalls his first meeting with Brother Holmes: "When I met Terry he was wearing a pair of dark glasses. I had no idea that he wore them regularly and that we were in the process of calling a missionary who was nearly blind to be quality control inspector on the temple project!"[1]

When the Holmeses were set apart, Terry received a promise that he would regain his vision. "I could feel within my heart," Brother Holmes later recorded, "the spirit of the work I needed to accomplish over the next few years."[2]

Brother Rowley noticed that "Elder Holmes' health [became] a concern to everyone but him. He never complained about his health difficulties, which included a restricted diet, heart monitoring, and cancer. He insisted that no matter how uncomfortable he was feeling when he awoke each morning, he would feel better when he came to the temple site. This always seemed to be the case. Even his eyesight was restored from near blindness to the point where he could drive to and from work."[3]

One of the greatest blessings of their mission, according to Sister Holmes, was Brother Holmes's restored health. Indeed, the Lord blessed Elder and Sister Holmes with the physical strength and health to fulfill their responsibilities. They labored over forty hours a week at the temple site and often had to be reminded at night that it was time to go home. They were among those who made the Houston Texas Temple as perfect as it could be.

There were many miracles, both dramatic and subtle, associated with the building of the Houston Texas Temple. One miracle may have seemed an obstacle at first. Because the temple is built on a floodplain, special care was taken to ensure that the building met floodplain regulations. In a three-month period, the temple site was flooded three times. But the builders weren't at all bothered by the floods. Instead, the excess water provided builders with information on how to build up the site and adequately protect the temple from imminent flooding after its completion.[4]

AMERICA'S FOUNDING FATHERS

St. George Utah Temple

Perhaps the best known story associated with temple work for the dead occurred in the St. George Utah Temple. President Wilford Woodruff was in the temple late one evening when the spirits of many of America's Founding Fathers gathered around him. He testified that "every one of those men that signed the Declaration of Independence, with General Washington, called upon me as an Apostle of the Lord Jesus Christ, in the Temple at St. George, two consecutive nights, and demanded at my hands that I should go forth and attend to ordinances of the House of God for them."[1]

On August 21, 1877, President Woodruff was baptized by Elder John D. T. McAllister for one hundred persons, including all the signers of the Declaration of Independence except two (John Hancock and William Floyd), whose ordinance work had already been done. President Woodruff then baptized Elder McAllister for twenty-one men, including George Washington and his forefathers and all the presidents of the United States for whom President Woodruff had not been baptized, except three (James Buchanan, Martin Van Buren, and Ulysses S. Grant), whose work has since been completed. Sister Lucy Bigelow Young was baptized for Martha Washington and female members of her family, as well as seventy other eminent women. Later that week the men were ordained elders—except George Washington, John Wesley, Benjamin Franklin, and

Christopher Columbus, who were ordained high priests—in preparation for the endowment ceremony, which was likewise performed by proxy for them.[2]

President Wilford Woodruff shared his feelings about these sacred events at general conference on April 10, 1898: "I am going to bear my testimony to this assembly, if I never do it again in my life, that those men who laid the foundation of this American government and signed the Declaration of Independence were the best spirits the God of heaven could find on the face of the earth. They were choice spirits, not wicked men. George Washington and all the men that labored for the purpose were inspired of the Lord."[3]

A MOST SACRED EXPERIENCE

Salt Lake Temple

President Wilford Woodruff's health had slowly been failing for some time before he passed away at age 91 on September 2, 1898. Days before his passing it became apparent that his time to leave mortality was drawing near. As president of the Quorum of the Twelve Apostles, Lorenzo Snow knew the mantle of leadership would pass to him upon the prophet's death, and he was greatly troubled at this prospect.

One evening President Snow dressed in his temple robes and entered the most holy of the Salt Lake Temple's rooms, where he entreated the Lord to spare President Woodruff's life.

Days later, President Snow received word of the prophet's passing. Again, in special prayer within the temple walls, President Snow poured out his heart to the Lord. He reminded the Lord how he had once asked that he might never be called upon to bear the heavy burdens and responsibilities of leading the Church. "Nevertheless," he said, "Thy will, be done. I have not sought this responsibility but if it be Thy will, I now present myself before Thee for Thy guidance and instruction. I ask that Thou show me what Thou wouldst have me do."[1]

His supplication was not immediatly answered. He left the room, passing into a large corridor. There, President Snow received a glorious manifestation. A granddaughter, Allie Young Pond, recorded this experience:

"One evening when I was visiting Grandpa Snow in his room in the Salt Lake Temple, I remained until the doorkeepers had gone and the nightwatchman had not yet come in, so Grandpa said he would take me to the main front entrance and let me out that way. He got his bunch of keys from his dresser.

"After we left his room and while we were still in the large corridor, leading into the celestial room, I was walking several steps ahead of Grandpa when he stopped me, saying: 'Wait a moment, Allie. I want to tell you something. It was right here that the Lord Jesus Christ appeared to me at the time of the death of President Woodruff. He instructed me to go right ahead and reorganize the First Presidency of the Church at once and not wait as he had done after the death of the previous presidents, and that I was to succeed President Woodruff.'

"Then Grandpa came a step nearer and held out his left hand and said: 'He stood right here, about three feet above the floor. It looked as though He stood on a plate of solid gold.'

"Grandpa told me what a glorious personage the Savior is and described His hands, feet, countenance and beautiful White Robes, all of which were of such a glory of whiteness and brightness that he could hardly gaze upon Him.

"Then Grandpa came another step nearer me and put his right hand on my head and said: 'Now, granddaughter, I want you to remember that this is the testimony of your grandfather, that he told you with his own lips that he actually saw the Savior here in the Temple and talked with Him face to face.'"[2]

A CHANGE OF HEART

Copenhagen Denmark Temple

The temple is literally the house of the Lord, a holy sanctuary where sacred ordinances are performed for both the living and the dead. Satan and his fallen angels are acutely aware of the temple's vital role in the salvation of man. Thus, through generations of time, they have stirred up the hearts of many men and distracted and misled others as they have worked to impede the progress of temples. Frequently, the most visible and unfortunate time of opposition occurs during a temple's public open house. During this time of celebration, antagonists frequently carry signs, shout phrases, distribute literature, and occasionally require law-enforced restraint.

Amidst such opposition, a significant change of attitude occurred among an entire neighborhood near the Copenhagen Denmark Temple. Many of the neighbors in the apartment buildings that surround the temple had significant problems with the temple's construction. Sister Rita Jensen, a temple construction missionary, recalled how she often heard comments such as, "The noise, the dust, why is this taking so long?"

The neighbors were the first people to visit the temporary visitors' center established on the sidewalk in front of the temple. Initially, the neighbors used the center to vent their frustrations. Sister Jensen, who frequently served in the center, remembers that "after a while there was no anger any more. The same people became interested and enthusiastic about the project. They would ask, 'How is it going? Are you going to finish on time?' We developed great friendships with the neighbors; in fact, the neighbors became our best missionaries because they were handing out the 'pass-along cards.' They would come back and ask for more because they had already handed out all their supply. They were excited about the temple and referred to the temple as 'their temple.' They were proud of it and how it turned out. They commented on how much they enjoyed the flowers and how the neighborhood is now so beautiful. It was kind of funny: whenever a new phase of construction began, they would immediately come into the visitors' center to get an update on what was happening next. We even had the neighbors bring us candy and flowers; they were so nice to us. The neighbors have taken pride in the temple and we believe that they will help keep a watchful eye on the temple."[1]

CARJACKED AND KIDNAPPED

Aba Nigeria Temple

The faithful Nigerian Saints had waited for many years for a temple in their homeland, and the Church was eager to complete the Nigerian temple. As a member of the Church's Temple Construction Department, Lynn Higginson was responsible for early stages of construction on the Aba Nigeria Temple. A series of problems had delayed construction, so Brother Higginson was asked to travel to Aba and remedy any unresolved issues.

In February 2001, Brother Higginson ventured to Africa for the first time in his life. After a lengthy journey, he arrived at the Lagos Nigeria International Airport and was met by Aba Nigeria Temple architect Dr. Simon Coker. What happened next to Brother Higginson is amazing and miraculous:

"We stacked the luggage in back of a silver-gray Peugeot 505 station wagon. We didn't give thought to the fact that our luggage was visible to others as we maneuvered through jammed traffic exiting the airport.

"I had never seen so much pedestrian traffic mixed so intimately with so much vehicular traffic. In the city of thirteen million, the traffic on the streets and highways is virtually ungoverned. Except for a very few scattered exceptions, there are no traffic lights, no stop signs, no center lines, no painted traffic lanes, no speed limits, no respected rights-of-way, and virtually no traffic law enforcement. Every commercial means of transportation was jammed so tightly that all doors and windows were left open to accommodate protruding arms, heads, and bodies, some even clinging on from the outside. Motorbikes could be seen with up to six on board. Every vehicle had one thing in common: an incessantly working horn that warned others to make way or keep their distance. Right-of-way goes to drivers with nerves of steel.

"I was so astonished at the sights I was witnessing that I was oblivious to attentions paid to us. A white man traveling with three black men made us somewhat conspicuous. While engulfed in my many observations, I did not mention to my traveling companions that a silver Mercedes Benz . . . occupied only by the driver, had been driving near us despite the chaotic traffic. At times the Mercedes was behind us, at times beside us, and often ahead of us. With my experience in life, I couldn't conceive that a car in front of us could be 'tailing us.'

"As we exited off the road, I noticed the silver Mercedes was to our left, about a half car length in front of us, and it began to pull into our lane. Our driver braked hard, hit his horn, and crowded the barrier to our right, but the Mercedes kept coming, made contact, and stopped, wedging us to a stop against the curb. I thought I had just seen the typical fender-bender that I had been expecting to see ever since leaving the airport. Simon leaped out to confront the reckless driver, but he met a gunman coming from the front of the Mercedes instead. The gunman ordered Simon into the back seat. The gunman climbed into the front passenger seat, reached across the car, and unlocked the driver-side door. An accomplice opened the driver's door and ordered our driver to the middle, where he had to sit on the emergency brake handle. Our new driver yanked the car into gear and sped past the yielding Mercedes. He kept the pedal clear to the floor, and with the gear shift remaining in second gear, the engine screamed. Traffic was lighter and the young criminal careened back and forth avoiding collisions. I was terrified the driver might crash the car, or worse, that the gunman might shoot us. *This is real,* I thought. We had been carjacked and kidnapped.

"While we sped down the road, the gunman proceeded to rob us. First, he asked for our money. He then ordered us to hand over our wrist watches. Both young men, the driver and the gunman, were extremely nervous, and seemed to be in a dreadful hurry. We handed over our watches. After examining them, he handed them back. Then he demanded our passports. We later deduced from this that they must have observed our arrival at the airport.

"I was praying silently while I studied the face of the gunman for any hint of his intentions. *Father,* I prayed, *I am on Thy errand, doing Thy work. It is up to Thee to protect us so we might complete our assignment.*

"We approached the end of a long bridge. The driver braked hard and pulled over to the right railing. 'Get out!' the gunman ordered. I thought, 'Oh, no! They will search me, and when they find I have concealed my wallet, it will make them mad enough to shoot me!' But to my relief, they only sped away in the stolen car containing all our luggage. Simon used his cell phone to call his family, who sent a car to rescue us. When it came, we drove on and found to our tremendous relief, our abandoned Peugeot with all our luggage intact and undisturbed.

"My greatest loss was my American passport, which sells on the black market for a million naira ($10,000). But thanks to the American Embassy, and some miraculous assistance from Heavenly Father, I obtained a replacement passport. Besides that, I only lost $19 and my son's money clip. What I gained was a greater love for my Heavenly Father. We kept every one of our appointments . . . on schedule . . . and carried out every part of our assignment."[1]

The Aba Nigeria Temple was dedicated in August 2005.

Aside from the Salt Lake Temple, the Aba Nigeria Temple is likely the most secured temple in the Church. The perimeter of the temple complex is protected by ten- to fourteen-foot-high gates, walls, and fences. Razor-sharp metal is attached to the top of the walls, preventing anyone from successfully climbing over. Twelve powerful cameras survey all angles of the temple complex twenty-four hours a day. These cameras are monitored and controlled within the gate house. Multiple professional security personnel continually staff various positions to protect the temple and secure the safety of temple visitors.[2]

A BEACON IN THE HURRICANE

Apia Samoa Temple

In December 1991, one of the worst tropical storms in recent history pummeled the islands of Western and American Samoa for five days. The storm, named Hurricane Val, was particularly discouraging because after pounding the islands for two days, it seemed to weaken, which provided people with a false sense of relief. The storm then turned a full loop and hit the islands again from different directions, with even stronger winds. The storm killed at least seventeen people and damaged or destroyed more than 65 percent of the homes on the islands. Roads, hospitals, a fire station, and virtually all the islands' crops were destroyed. Downed telephone and utility lines made communication difficult.[1]

When the storm ended, it was found that all sixty-nine of the Church's meetinghouses in Western Samoa had sustained some damage; and most of the meetinghouses in American Samoa received major damage. Despite the havoc raging around it, the Apia Samoa Temple was protected, receiving a relatively small amount of water damage. Additionally, due to emergency generators, a light on the temple's tower shone brightly during the storm. One member said: "It was about the only light in the whole end of the island. It stood out as a beacon in the storm."[2]

MANY HANDS MAKE LIGHT WORK

Baton Rouge Louisiana Temple

In June 2000, the Baton Rouge Louisiana Temple was ready to be faced with Imperial Danby white marble. Many of the smaller temples built at the time—including the temple in Baton Rouge—used this beautiful marble, acquired from a quarry near Sharon, Vermont, birthplace of the Prophet Joseph Smith.

Truckloads of the beautiful white stone were arriving daily. One evening, an eighteen-wheel truck arrived at the construction site after hours. Only the marble foreman was still on site to receive the shipment of ten crates of marble, each weighing three-quarters of a ton. The foreman unloaded two crates with a forklift before a hydraulic line on it broke, rendering the machine useless.

A few phone calls were made, and within fifteen minutes twenty-five strong young men were there, ready to assist with the seemingly insurmountable task. The truck driver made an attempt to help the situation by backing the truck closer to the temple. But in doing so, he managed only to get stuck in a pile of sand. The young men went to work and unloaded the remaining eight crates, totaling approximately fifteen thousand pounds of marble. They then went the extra mile by placing the marble, piece by piece, around the temple where workers could use it as it was needed. Through the entire process, only one piece of marble was broken.

After transporting all the marble, the young men focused their efforts on freeing the stranded truck. In a unified effort of strength, they managed to rock the big semitruck off the sand pile. All of the evening's diligent labors required only one and one-half hour's time.

Temple construction missionary Weldon Smith believes the Lord gave the young men extra strength to complete their worthy task. Elder Smith said, "The young men received a great blessing by being able to provide useful labor on the temple. Someday, they will share this wonderful story with their children."[1]

PETITIONING FOR A TEMPLE

Billings Montana Temple

To gain access to services such as water, sewer, electric power, and natural gas, the Billings Temple committee found it necessary to ask the city council to annex the temple site. Nearly 1,200 people attended a city council meeting in support of annexation. Despite the impressive turnout, the council made a surprising move and denied the request.

Church members quickly organized a petition drive to persuade the city council to reconsider the request for annexation. Sister Susan Smith, who was asked to organize the drive, recorded: "I sought direction by means of prayer in the work that was about to begin, and the Spirit testified to me how this work was to be done. . . . More than four hundred members of the Church—men, women, teenagers, and children—labored with love as they gathered signatures of support from the community. The drive was successful beyond merely gathering thousands of signatures in that it gave Church members a chance to talk with hundreds of people about concerns related to the temple and misconceptions about the LDS Church. . . .

"As more petition signatures came in, cheers of joy erupted and tears were shed. Church members had gathered nearly ten thousand signatures over the weekend! Exhausted, many labored all night and into the morning to complete the recording and get copies of the signatures run off to present to each member of the city council the next day. We made a presentation and explained our labor of love to many of the city council members. Some accepted with appreciation and others with doubt, but in our hearts we knew we had accomplished the wishes of our Heavenly Father."[1]

This heroic petition drive played a key role in persuading the city council to vote 8 to 3 in approval of the annexation.

The announcement of the Billings Montana Temple brought with it a flood of negative publicity for the Church and the temple. Less than a month after the temple's announcement, "The Rimrock Task Force" was formed to oppose the temple and its position near the city's rimrock formations. Attempting to cause alarm, the task force published exaggerated photos, demonstrating how the proposed temple would block the natural beauty of the rims. These photos displayed a superimposed photograph of the Washington D.C. Temple from a low angle, making it appear to tower in front of the rims.

The Church made many concessions to appease citizen concerns. This included structural modifications to the temple, reducing the intensity of temple lighting, and coloring perimeter walls to match the indigenous color of the rims.[2]

THE FIRST PRESIDENCY AND A FIRE CHIEF

Boise Idaho Temple

During the open house for the Boise Idaho Temple in 1984, Church officials worked to obtain an occupancy permit to accommodate the many Saints who wanted to attend the fast-approaching dedicatory services. The projected number of attendees far exceeded the number deemed reasonable by Boise's fire-safety codes.

Early one morning, architect Ronald W. Thurber called the city's fire chief and invited him to a personally guided tour of the entire temple. An appointment was made for 10 A.M. that day. Brother Thurber immediately notified Elder Hugh W. Pinnock of the First Quorum of the Seventy, the General Authority assisting with the temple, who agreed to arrive at the temple half an hour early. As Brother Thurber, Elder Pinnock, and other Church officials gathered in the temple president's office, Elder Pinnock told the others that he had called the First Presidency in Salt Lake City that morning and told them of the challenge. The First Presidency had put the item on the prayer roll that day and would be praying during their weekly meeting in the temple, which happened to coincide with Brother Thurber's tour with the fire chief.

At 10 A.M. the fire chief arrived and was given a private tour of the temple. Afterward, he agreed to grant the temple a permit for unlimited occupancy, as long as a few safety procedures were followed. After the fire chief drove away,

BOISE IDAHO TEMPLE

the group returned to the president's office to give a prayer of thanks. Brother Thurber was asked to pray and later said, "I was in such tears I could hardly pray. The First Presidency had taken a particular issue and solved it by imploring the assistance of Heavenly Father."[1]

After the Boise Idaho Temple was completed, some neighbors were upset at the intense lighting used on the temple after dusk. In an effort to calm their complaints, temple lighting was reduced. The reduction in light, however, resulted in temple officials receiving phone calls from the local airport requesting that the lights be turned back on. According to Ronald W. Thurber, architect of the Boise Temple, "We found out later that airplanes making their final approach to the Boise Airport use the temple as a visual reference landmark because it is so well lit at night."[2]

"I AM HER CHILD"

Cardston Alberta Temple

During a dedicatory session of the Cardston Alberta Temple in 1923, President Heber J. Grant said: "I want to bear my witness here today in connection with others, that the unseen powers, that those who are working for us beyond the veil, never lose their interest in the work of those who are living here upon the earth."[1]

Since that time, many temple workers and patrons in the Cardston Alberta Temple have experienced strong spiritual manifestations while performing saving ordinances for themselves and the deceased. Here is one:

"Mrs. Newlun from Portland, a convert to the Church, was in a sealing room [of the Alberta Temple] to be sealed to her dead husband and to have their dead children sealed to them. Friends were to act as proxy for the husband and children.

"As President Wood was ready to seal the children to the parents, he said he felt impressed to ask if the information on the sealing sheet was complete. After being assured that the record was right, he again began the ceremony. He said he again felt impressed to ask if she had other children whose names should be on the sheet. She said she had other living adult children who were not members of the Church and hence their names should not be included. The third time the President started the ceremony, whereupon he stopped and said, 'I

heard a voice quite distinctly saying "I am her child."' He again asked the mother if she had another child that was not on the sheet. She answered, with tears running down her face, 'Yes, I had another daughter who died when twelve days old and she was overlooked in preparing the information.' When the group learned how the President knew of the other child, all in the room shed tears of joy to know of the apparent nearness of our kindred dead."[2]

UNIFYING TWO NATIONS

Ciudad Juárez Mexico Temple

The Ciudad Juárez Mexico Temple serves Latter-day Saints on both sides of the United States–Mexico border. Ciudad Juárez, Mexico's fourth largest city, is located across the Rio Grande River, less than thirty miles from El Paso, Texas. The temple was built in Ciudad Juárez rather than El Paso because it is relatively easy for citizens of the United States to travel from El Paso into Mexico, but it is very difficult for most Mexican citizens to travel into the United States.

When the temple was first announced, however, members living in the United States were apprehensive about traveling into Mexico. Well-established beliefs and dangerous conditions in Juárez had prevented many members from ever traveling south across the border. Over a short period of time, though, the temple brought together members on both sides of the border, despite the differences in nations and cultures.

In an effort to make El Paso members more comfortable with traveling to the temple, Church leaders planned weekly excursions to visit the temple during its construction period. American members quickly became familiar with the direct route to the temple, how to cross the border, and where some of the most popular restaurants were located.

As the temple neared completion, members of both communities helped ensure that brothers and sisters in need had temple clothing. Some members donated extra or new clothing; many loaned their own. Groups of sisters from El Paso traveled across the border to help their Mexican sisters make temple clothing and slippers. During the final weeks of construction, Church members from the United States and Mexico worked in partnership on the temple site daily. This labor of love included landscaping, cleaning both the interior and exterior of the temple, and washing windows. It was calculated that members donated more than fifty thousand hours of work on the temple. Construction missionaries Elder Richard Skidmore and Sister Bon Adell Skidmore witnessed the loving cooperation of the cultures, saying, "We feel like there has been more than a temple built here. We have witnessed a mingling of cultures and a sharing of ideas."[1]

PEACE AMID POLITICAL UNREST

Cochabamba Bolivia Temple

The Cochabamba Bolivia Temple stands prominently in a city with a worthy heritage and wonderful people. When the temple neared completion, however, a darker chapter of the nation's history was unfolding. Escalating political, social, and economic tensions came to a climax on April 8, 2000, when Bolivia's president declared a state of emergency. Tension throughout the country and exploding rebellion in Cochabamba was caused by increasing utility prices. Police were dispatched into the streets with anti-riot gear, tear gas, and rubber bullets in an effort to squelch the unrest.

The temple's highly anticipated open house became an overwhelming challenge due to obvious safety concerns. As a precautionary measure, Church officials decided to reduce the two-week-long open house to one week. The reduced time allotted for the Saints to take part in these activities created larger groups participating in the remaining open house tours. Despite these changes, Church officials were wonderfully surprised at the attendance.

According to Brother Enrique O. Huerta of the Cochabamba Bolivia Universidad Stake: "We were supposed to be under martial law for 90 days, but it was lifted after 13 days. We anticipated 50,000 visitors in two weeks of [the] open house, but instead, we got 65,570 in one week. Twenty thousand people came in one day. They were lined up for blocks and stayed until midnight."[1]

DAD'S MILLENNIUM DAY LILIES

Columbus Ohio Temple

Among the eighteen varieties of trees, shrubs, perennials, and ground cover surrounding the Columbus Ohio Temple is a noteworthy flower donated by the family of Donald Werling. "One of dad's greatest desires," his daughter says, "was to have his day lilies beautify the temple grounds." As the owner of a flower business, he had mastered the hybridization process and created his own variety, which he named the Millennium Day Lily. When he tried to register the name, however, he found that the name had already been used. From then on, his family affectionately referred to his special lilies as *Dad's* Millennium Day Lilies.

As landscaping plans were being made for the temple, Brother Werling was devastated by a nearly fatal heart attack, which left him permanently disabled. Although he could no longer work with his flowers, his family decided to pursue his dream of supplying the temple with these unique lilies. A few weeks before the temple's open house, Church members arrived early in the morning to begin the enormous task of planting five hundred clusters of the special lilies. The volunteers lovingly carried out each step of the repetitive task involved in planting the lilies. The temple's landscape architect referred to the lilies as a legacy of Donald Werling.[1]

As the temple construction committee began to discuss architectural aspects of the Columbus Ohio Temple, many agreed that there should be a visible tie between the Kirtland and Columbus Temples. It was finally determined that the east window of the upper court in the Kirtland Temple— known as the "Window Beautiful"—would be a perfect way to symbolically connect the two Ohio temples. This window was designed by Salt Lake Temple architect Truman Angell.

Brother Brent Harris, known for his skill in carpentry, was given the responsibility to authentically replicate this historic window. Of this opportunity, Brother Harris said, "I couldn't believe I was actually going to be able to help build a temple, and now to be able to construct a replica of the Window Beautiful was beyond my dreams. All I can say is that it was a real privilege to be able to accept and finish this assignment."[2] Of all the temple's outward features, the Window Beautiful is the most spectacular.

TEMPERING THE WEATHER

Detroit Michigan Temple

As construction on the Detroit Michigan Temple progressed, the Saints prayed that Michigan's traditionally harsh winter weather would be moderated and thus facilitate the work. Workers began pouring concrete for the temple's foundation in January and continued to do so through the cold and snowy months that followed. To allow the concrete to set properly, it had to be covered and heated for several days until it had properly cured. Temple construction missionary Elder Keith Brown said, "As cold as it was, I do not think that we ever had weather severe enough to interrupt construction."[1]

A miracle also occurred on the day the temple walls were put in place. The walls were assembled flat on the ground and then hoisted by a crane into position. Elder Brown described the experience: "The day the crane arrived the area was experiencing thirty-mile-an-hour winds. But on the building site, it was never too windy to set the walls. Can you imagine a forty-foot wall, twenty feet high, in a thirty-mile-an-hour wind? On the site it was not that windy and we set all the walls in one day."[2]

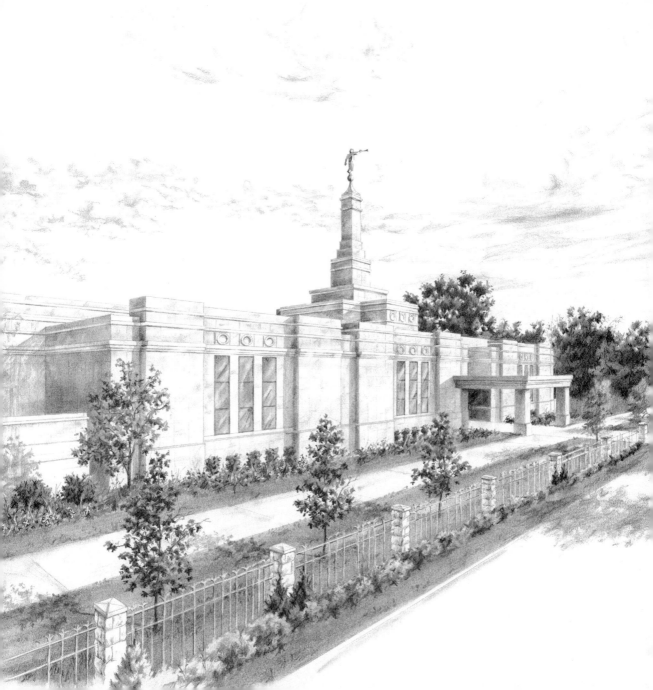

In 1956 the Church bought nearly eight acres of land for construction of the Detroit area's first stake center. The land not used by the stake center was never sold and became the location for the Detroit Michigan Temple. As soon as temple construction began, the temple became an important feature in the lives of area members, including Primary children. During all phases of the construction, the children attending the meetinghouse adjacent to the temple grounds would look out their window toward the temple and sing, "I Love to See the Temple." Primary children contributed by saving their pennies and putting them into a bank—a hollow wooden replica of the temple. Their sincere efforts resulted in a contribution of nearly two hundred dollars to their temple.[3]

A SPECIAL DREAM

Houston Texas Temple

Richard Gieseke, a Church member and owner of a small landscaping nursery in Houston, played a special role in beautifying the grounds of the Houston Texas Temple.

One night, a few months before the temple was announced, he dreamed of gardens adorning an unknown temple. "The dream was so vivid," he recorded, "that I awoke and wrote a letter to the First Presidency of the Church and filed it for later use. The unusual dream was of a beautiful temple with lovely gardens in special arrangements. From the dream I knew the Lord wanted me to begin growing plants at my nursery for the temple."[1]

And he did just that, using his filed-away letter when the temple was announced three months after his dream.

Six months before his dream, Brother Gieseke had unexpectedly acquired 100 four-year-old oaks. For a reason he cannot explain, he planted the trees in containers larger than usual. After the dream, he designated the finest of the oaks and the best of his other plant material exclusively for future temple grounds. He made every effort to ensure that his temple stock were of "uncommon excellence." As time passed, his specially designated temple plants grew in size, quality, and value. On many occasions he had opportunities to sell the trees to fill orders that were otherwise unfillable, but he remained firm in his decision that these plants were for the temple. Other miraculous events occurred in his business to allow him to purchase and grow additional plants and trees. In August 1998, for example, he received a call from a construction foreman, offering him thirty large crape myrtles that were about to be destroyed by a bulldozer. In one-hundred-degree heat, four twenty-five-foot myrtles in ground as hard as concrete were carefully excavated. To prevent them from dehydrating, they were stripped of all their leaves and small branches and planted in massive 200-gallon buckets. The three-day effort under an extreme Texas sun was not in vain; to everyone's relief, all of the myrtles survived the transplants.

In retrospect, Brother Gieseke recognizes how he and his nursery business were blessed during this several-year period. Just before he had his dream, his nursery had consisted of six acres. Within a few years he had the opportunity to acquire a prosperous forty-acre nursery and a fifty-acre tree farm. Brother Gieseke attests, "Because of the Lord's blessings, a six-acre nursery, too small to accommodate and donate all the temple plants, tripled its volume and became a 96-acre business. It is true the Lord will open the windows of heaven to pour out His blessings. I have seen this firsthand. I have been blessed many times over the dollar amount donated to the temple, and I continue to be in debt to the Lord."[2]

The plant stock Brother Gieseke nurtured for the Lord's house finally had a permanent home on the grounds of the Houston Texas Temple in the year 2000, three years after his dream. The crape myrtles he had rescued were the exact color of white myrtle needed to provide contrasting color against the temple's gray granite exterior. These majestic trees now stand at the front of the temple's entryway. Brother Gieseke said, "I feel that this experience has been the highlight of my career. I thank God that He gave me a special dream that empowered me with the desire to get involved in an eternal undertaking."[3]

THE CRANE THAT ALMOST TOPPLED

Kona Hawaii Temple

Nearly everyone involved in building a temple witnesses a miracle or two along the way. Brother Myron Lindsey, who worked on the Kona Hawaii Temple, is such an individual. One day Brother Lindsey was moving more than two tons of rebar to the temple site with a mobile crane. He had to reposition the crane so he could put the rebar down inside the building. But the ground was soft and not at all compact. The crane started to sink in the loose ground; and because of a heavy load up front, it began to topple on two wheels. Brother Lindsey feared he would have to jump out of the machine and watch it careen to the ground. But somehow the crane came to a halt at its apex and slowly came back down to a leveling position on its four wheels. "I did nothing to the crane," he told a missionary serving as temple historian. "It straightened itself back up. There were people working down below that would have been hurt or killed if it had turned over. I was praying very hard at the time. Heavenly Father loves me. There were three witnesses to this event."[1]

A SHIPWRECK AND SALVAGED LUMBER

Laie Hawaii Temple

When the Laie Hawaii Temple was built in the early 1900s, the island of Oahu was quite remote. This made it difficult to receive shipments of building materials, such as lumber and other supplies. Several creative means were employed to get around the problem. For example, crushed lava and coral—both easily available on the island—were added to the concrete that was used to form the entire edifice, including the floors, ceilings, walls, and roof.[1]

But even with this innovation, construction often had to wait while contractors tried to locate missing materials. At one point, construction was at a standstill due to lack of lumber. Contractor Ralph Woolley prayed for help in obtaining the needed supplies. Two days later, during a severe storm, a freight ship was stranded on a nearby coral reef. The captain offered the Saints his cargo of lumber if they would help him unload his ship. The Saints agreed, and thus work on the temple could be resumed.

When Ray E. Dillman served as president of the Laie Hawaii Temple from 1956 to 1960, the white temple was painted a shade of pale green. The new color was meant to blend better with the surrounding landscape. Instead, the color proved a shock to many who saw it. Within a few years, the pale green faded and the temple was restored to its glistening white appearance.[2]

PRESIDENT TAYLOR AND THE SPIRIT OF DISCERNMENT

Logan Utah Temple

In Nauvoo, the Prophet Joseph Smith said to Elder John Taylor: "Elder Taylor, you have received the Holy Spirit and if you are faithful in heeding its promptings the day will come when it will be within you a fountain of continuous revelation from God."[1]

One such day came during a dedicatory session for the Logan Utah Temple in May 1884. John Taylor was then President of the Church and was watching as hundreds of people entered the temple. He suddenly turned to Stake President Charles O. Card and said that a certain woman coming through the doorway was not worthy to enter the temple. Although she possessed a seemingly valid recommend, she was escorted out of the temple without raising much opposition.

Following the dedicatory services, President Taylor told President Card and several others, "Brethren, you may deceive the Bishop and you may deceive the Presidents of the Stake, and you may deceive the General authorities of the Church, but you cannot deceive the Lord Jesus Christ nor the Holy Ghost. You know yourselves better than anybody else and if there is anything wrong in you, now is the time to repent and make yourselves square with the Lord; and if you do not repent, the time will come when you will be humbled, and the higher up you get the greater will be your fall."[2]

Later, President Card visited the lady at her home and inquired how she had obtained her recommend. He discovered that this woman had purchased the recommend for a dollar from a man who himself was unworthy to have a recommend. Although President Taylor had never seen this woman before, the Spirit had whispered that of the 2,000 people in attendance, she was not worthy to be there.

FLOWERING OF FAITH

Madrid Spain Temple

Interior designer Aubrey Conner experienced a "flowering of faith" while working on the floral arrangements for the Madrid Spain Temple.

The silk flowers selected for the temple came in two shipments, each arriving on a different day. Because Brother Conner was short on time, he began arranging the flowers with only the first shipment, which meant setting aside some of his original plans—and some of the flowers that had arrived in the first shipment. Still, he managed to create a number of beautiful arrangements with the flowers he had.

"Later," he writes, "when the second shipment arrived, I discovered that the flowers for the celestial room were missing. They never showed up. So we traveled throughout Madrid to locate a good source for artificial flowers. None existed, and time was running out. I panicked, and I remember one of the ladies who had accompanied me saying, 'Brother Conner, you are always preaching about faith and how things will always work together for our good. Now where is your faith?'

"The situation seemed so hopeless and impossible to solve. We prayed that a solution would present itself. When I unpacked the rest of the second shipment, I discovered the flowers that I had eliminated from the first day's arrangements. Interestingly enough, they were all white and pastel formal flowers that

TEMPLO DE MADRID
LA IGLESIA DE JESUCRISTO DE LOS SANTOS DE LOS ÚLTIMOS DÍAS

proved to be perfect for the celestial room arrangements. I have come to real-ize that this is the Lord's work and that even though things might go wrong, he will always provide a solution if we exercise a little faith."[1]

Arranging flowers for a temple is a complicated and time-consuming endeavor. Before beginning, temple floral designers consider the building's floor plan, architectural details, specified furnishings, fabrics, wall coverings, and lighting. The shape, size, and color of each floral masterpiece is designed to fit in a specific location. The spiritual significance of each room in the temple is also reflected in the flowers. For example, flowers that flourish near water sources are often used in the baptistry.

AN INTERNATIONALLY DIVERSE TEMPLE

Manhattan New York Temple

New York City Church members are internationally diverse, reflecting the city's "crossroads of the world" reputation. Wards or branches are conducted in English, Spanish, Chinese, Korean, and American Sign Language. The New York New York North and South Missions, both headquartered in the city, stock the Book of Mormon in eighty languages.[1] Ordinance workers who serve in the Manhattan New York Temple reflect these diverse demographics. Temple patrons are faithfully served by workers from at least twenty-four different countries, including India, Romania, Jamaica, Nigeria, the Philippines, China, Haiti, Vietnam, and Australia, to name a few. These delightful servants bring with them vastly different languages, cultures, and backgrounds. But they also unite in loving the Lord and providing charitable service in His house.

Certainly, there is a celestial feeling of brotherhood and sisterhood in the Manhattan Temple. The temple workers are frequently presented with opportunities to use their language and cultural backgrounds to assist temple visitors and make them feel more at home in the temple.

Full-time temple missionaries Brent M. Cederlof and his wife, Wendy, were among the first group of missionaries to serve in the Manhattan Temple. For the entire duration of their mission they marveled at how this unique group of workers was able to bless the patrons and enhance the spirit of the temple. Brother

Cederlof recalls one occasion when they "had a large and unusual session, consisting of thirty-seven sisters and ten brothers. Among them were ten Spanish speaking, five Chinese, four Mandarin, and one Cantonese. I felt very emotional to observe as sisters and brothers were assisted in their own languages into the celestial room." He later made the observation: "New York is one of the last major cities in the world to have a temple. The Lord has prepared a way for this temple to effectively serve temple visitors originating from many different countries and cultures. I have seen people from far away countries arrive at the temple and be greeted by someone from their country; . . . it just means everything to them. People have been brought together who can handle just about anything and anyone. It is a beautiful thing. I can see the hand of the Lord in how this temple staff has been brought together."[2]

Most temples in the world allow for temple visitors to drive to the temple, park their cars, and take a leisurely walk past beautiful landscaping and fountains as they approach the doors of the temple. This allows the temple patrons a few moments to redirect their thoughts and prepare to enter the house of the Lord. The Manhattan Temple, however, is a complete contrast to the traditional temple setting. The doors of the temple open directly onto busy and noisy Columbus Avenue, just a few feet from Broadway. Mere inches separate the spirit of the temple from the world outside. Walking from crowded streets through doors and immediately seeing the temple recommend desk can be a shocking experience, in a pleasant way, for guests of the temple. Temple missionary Brent M. Cederlof observed, "As people enter the temple they are frequently astounded at the difference they see and feel. Many people are so overwhelmed they shed tears upon entering. The sharp contrast emphasizes the difference between the temple and the world."[3]

The temple has a special feature that helps maintain its spirit. Although city noise never stops, it cannot be heard within the walls of the temple. Extensive design and construction techniques were implemented to create a building within a building. The soundproofed inner shell creates a quiet, serene atmosphere where members can enjoy peaceful reflection unique in New York City.

A SAVING DREAM

Manti Utah Temple

Edward L. Parry, master mason of the Manti Utah Temple dedicated in May 1888, was awakened one night during the temple's construction by a very realistic dream. In his dream, a man had fallen from the temple's scaffolding. Brother Parry awoke in a panic and immediately journeyed to the temple site. In the dark, he examined the scaffolding as best he could. His careful inspection revealed that an important support rope had worked itself loose. After making sufficient repairs, he returned home to his bed. Because he heeded the warning, no one was injured.[1]

The Manti Utah Temple boasts two grand, spiral stairways—each without a central support. These large stairways are two of only three of this type in the United States. Each staircase contains 151 steps, which support each other and are wide enough for four people to walk side-by-side, and 204 intricately fashioned spindles that support handcrafted black walnut railings. The staircase on the north circles clockwise and the one the south circles counterclockwise, each making six complete revolutions and reaching a vertical rise of 76 feet and 2¾ inches.[2]

PRESERVED DURING AN EARTHQUAKE

Oaxaca Mexico Temple

Because earthquakes are an ever-present possibility in southern Mexico, the temple in Oaxaca was built on pilings that make it as earthquake proof as possible. Two major earthquakes tested the temple before its construction was even complete. The first—a 6.5 quake with its epicenter two hundred miles north of Oaxaca—occurred in July 1999 as the temple's footings were being put into place. The next quake was much closer and more severe. On September 30, as the temple's exterior walls were nearing completion, a three-minute, 7.6 earthquake struck.

The temple's project manager, Jay Erekson, described the event: "As we were running out of the temple, the ground was bucking up and down six to eight inches. I stood there and watched as the windows went out of square in both directions. The temple's tower was whipping back and forth four or five feet. As I watched it happen, I started to cry because I thought, 'Our temple is ruined.' I thought we would have to tear it down and start over again."

More than one hundred buildings in the city were destroyed by the quake or damaged to the degree that they were later condemned. After the disaster, instruments were used to check every angle and line of the temple. "When we were through, we discovered that the temple had not moved a millimeter out of square or out of plumb. It was a miracle," said Brother Erekson.[1]

LAND PRESERVED FOR A TEMPLE

Bismarck North Dakota Temple

In 1976, the Church began looking for property on which to build a chapel for the Bismarck North Dakota Branch. The search team purchased a site that would accommodate future expansion—although the site had somewhat odd dimensions. The property was in the shape of the letter L, and some Saints in the area wondered what to do with the unused and seemingly useless leg of the property. Others felt confident that the piece of land would eventually serve a valuable purpose. Each time the Church considered selling the land, the district presidency received strong impressions that the land should not be sold; but they did not know why.

When the Bismarck North Dakota Temple was announced, the purpose for preserving this extra piece of land became clear. Unlike the seemingly endless delays and struggles that had been experienced while trying to acquire land for other temples throughout the world, very little effort was required for this temple to receive approval from the city. When the building permit request was submitted, the city employee simply asked, "You own the property, don't you?" The answer was affirmative. "Then we don't see a problem."

Lowell L. Cheney, a counselor in the stake presidency, shared his thoughts on these events: "Though individually each of these events may not have seemed exceptionally significant, an overview of what has transpired gives

profound assurance of the Lord's awareness of His children in this part of His vineyard and the desire for them to receive His choicest blessings. If we will but follow as directed by the Spirit, even though we may not see the whole picture, we can be confident that the work will go forth, for the Lord surely directs His work to completion."[1]

ROCKS OF FAITH

Redlands California Temple

As construction on the Redlands California Temple commenced, so did a program in the area inspired by the 2002 Primary theme, "I Love to See the Temple." Primary children began writing their names on individual rocks that would then be placed under the temple foundation. It was not long before members of all ages were submitting special rocks. Some rocks featured names, painted pictures, and messages in a number of languages. Some rocks were donated from the streambed at Glen Helen Regional Park in Devore, California, the campsite of LDS pioneers in 1851. In the end, more than 15,000 "temple rocks" were donated.[1]

"Rocks of Faith" projects have occurred during the construction of many of the Church's temples. Vernon Forbush, who served as project superintendent for both the Reno Nevada Temple and the Newport Beach California Temple, assisted members in placing thousands of pounds of rock beneath the baptismal fonts. While working on the Newport Beach Temple, Brother Forbush had the following experience: "In sacrament meeting one Sunday I saw two blind sisters. I thought to myself, 'They will never be able to clean the temple or participate in other ways. However, they can feel the rocks and place them in the foundation.' So arrangements were made to have them and their families place all the stones beneath the baptismal font."

Brother Forbush remembers two touching inscriptions written on rocks placed under the Reno Nevada Temple: "To baby Jessica, whom I was able to hold for a moment, may I live worthy enough to someday hold you for eternity." A little boy wrote, "I hope I am sealed in the temple someday if I am ever able to be adopted."[2]

NOTES

INTRODUCTION

    1. In Wendy O. Nielsen and Miken O. Johnson, *Gift of Love—The Houston Texas Temple* (Austin, Texas: Historical Publications, 2002), 116.

MUSIC STANDS AND SNOW SHOVELS

    1. In David G. Hein, "Temple ground made 'white and pure,'" *Church News*, April 4, 1998, 23.

    2. Jim Pottenger, interview by author, April 20, 2000.

THEY NAMED HIM TEMPLE

    1. In Donna and Vern Whisenant, "His Name Is Temple," *Meridian Magazine*, August 2005, http://www.ldsmag.com/churchupdate/050805templeprint.html

    2. As told by Howard and Esther Stratton, Aba Nigeria Temple construction missionaries, interview by author, audio recording, August 11, 2005.

    3. James E. Talmage, as quoted in Richard Neitzel Holzapfel, *Every Stone a Sermon* (Salt Lake City: Bookcraft, 1992), 82.

    4. See ibid.

SECURITY WATCHDOG

    1. See Phyllis and Bruce Belnap, Washington Temple Visitor Center (n.p.)

    2. See "To Build a Temple," *Ensign*, August 1974, 17.

TEMPLE SPARED DURING MILITARY CONFLICT

    1. Dallin H. Oaks, "Miracles," *Ensign*, June 2001, 16.

A MORMON PILGRIMAGE

    1. Howard L. Biddulph, *The Morning Breaks: Stories of Conversion and Faith in the Former Soviet Union* (Salt Lake City: Deseret Book, 1996), 180–81.

NOTES

2. Ibid., 186–88.

3. Ibid., 189–90.

DISCOVERING THE NAUVOO TEMPLE BLUEPRINTS

1. Marjorie H. Bennion, "The Rediscovery of William Weeks' Nauvoo Temple Drawings," *Mormon Historical Studies* 3, no. 1 (2002), 79–81.

2. Gordon B. Hinckley, "Thanks to the Lord for His Blessings," *Ensign*, May 1999, 89.

3. See J. Michael Hunter, "I Saw Another Angel Fly," *Ensign*, January 2000, 30.

THE HOUSE WAS GUARDED

1. Truman O. Angell, "Autobiography, Our Pioneer Heritage," in *Writings of Early Latter-day Saints*, comp. Milton V. Backman Jr. (Provo: Brigham Young University Department of Church History and Doctrine, 1996), 202–3.

A SPECIAL SESSION

1. See Gerry Avant, "Blessings of House of the Lord Reach Faithful in Many Lands," *Church News*, September 24, 1994, 27.

A TRAIL OF TEARS TO THE TEMPLE

1. Linda S. Stokes, "Finding My Choctaw Ancestors," *Ensign*, August 1988, 44.

2. Ibid.

3. Ibid., 44–45.

4. Ibid., 46.

5. Ibid.

REMEMBER THE ALAMO

1. See Ivan L. Hobson, *Dallas Texas Temple: An Early History* (Salt Lake City: Ivan Hobson, 1991), 128–29, 174.

LEARNING FROM MISTAKES

1. In Twila Bird, *Build unto My Holy Name: The Story of the Denver Temple* (Denver: Denver Colorado Area Public Communications Council, 1987), 12–13.

NOTES

2. In ibid., 16–17.

3. Joseph H. Barton, in ibid., 23.

4. Ibid., 28–29.

5. Kathleen P. Bullock, in ibid., 91–92.

Rolling in Snow

1. Thomas S. Monson, *Faith Rewarded: A Personal Account of Prophetic Promises to the East German Saints* (Salt Lake City: Deseret Book, 1996), 105.

2. Andreas Kleinert, as quoted in "Hero in the font," *Church News*, February 14, 1987, 16.

Spire Burnt to a Cinder

1. Herardo Rivera, interview by author, audio recording, trans. Adam Rigby, February 23, 2000.

2. Ibid.

The Lord Selects a Temple Site

1. In Nielsen and Johnson, *Gift of Love—The Houston Texas Temple*, 24; see also 21–24.

Many Ways to Contribute

1. David L. McKay and Mildred C. McKay, comp., *For His House* (Murray, Utah: Murray Utah Stake, 1978), 15.

2. See ibid., 13.

3. See ibid., 10.

4. In ibid., 27.

Future Temple Seen in a Dream

1. Philip Harris, interview by author, audio recording, January 22, 2000.

2. Ibid.

3. Ibid.

NOTES

CELESTIAL WINDOWS PROTECTED DURING EARTHQUAKE

1. See Richard and Linda Larkin, "Notes on the Las Vegas Temple," in Elbert B. Edwards, *The Las Vegas Temple* (privately published), 66.

A NEWSPAPER FROM ENGLAND

1. In *Our Heritage: A Brief History of The Church of Jesus Christ of Latter-day Saints* (Salt Lake City: The Church of Jesus Christ of Latter-day Saints, 1996), 99.

2. M. Russell Ballard, in "Missionary Journal: Five Church Leaders Look Back at Their British Isles Mission Experiences," *Ensign*, July 1987, 11.

AND THERE WAS LIGHT

1. Jay B. Jensen, personal recollections, unpublished manuscript, copy in author's possession.

2. Ibid.

AN ANGEL'S HALO

1. Juanee Baird, interview by author, audio recording, June 3, 2005.

DODGING A HURRICANE

1. Alaire Johnson, "Temple Project History," unpublished manuscript, copy in author's possession, 11.

OPEN THE BLIND EYES

1. In Nielsen and Johnson, *Gift of Love—The Houston Texas Temple*, 120.

2. In ibid., 122.

3. Ibid.

4. Ibid., 117.

AMERICA'S FOUNDING FATHERS

1. Wilford Woodruff, in Conference Report, April 1898, 89–90.

2. See *Wilford Woodruff's Journal*, ed. Scott G. Kenney, 9 vols. (Midvale, Utah: Signature Books, 1983–84), 7:367–69.

3. Woodruff, in Conference Report, April 1898, 89.

NOTES

A MOST SACRED EXPERIENCE

    1. In N. B. Lundwall, *Temples of the Most High* (Salt Lake City: Bookcraft, 1993), 40.
    2. Ibid., 141.

A CHANGE OF HEART

    1. Rita Jensen, interview by author, audio recording, April 29, 2004.

CARJACKED AND KIDNAPPED

    1. Adapted from Richard Lynn Higginson, unpublished personal history, copy in author's possession, used by permission.
    2. Stratton, interview.

A BEACON IN THE HURRICANE

    1. See "Hurricane Wreaks Ruin in Samoa," *Church News*, December 21, 1991, Z3.
    2. "Church Responds Swiftly to Samoa Disaster," *Church News*, December 28, 1991, Z14.

MANY HANDS MAKE LIGHT WORK

    1. Weldon Smith, interview by author, audio recording, September 12, 2000.

PETITIONING FOR A TEMPLE

    1. Susan Smith, in Joan R. Larsen, "History of the Billings Temple District," unpublished, 1999.
    2. Gale Mair, Billings Montana Temple project superintendent, interview by author, audio recording, April 12, 2000.

THE FIRST PRESIDENCY AND A FIRE CHIEF

    1. Ronald W. Thurber, interview by author, audio recording, September 26, 2000.
    2. Ibid.

"I AM HER CHILD"

    1. Heber J. Grant, as cited in V. A. Wood, *The Alberta Temple: Centre and Symbol of Faith* (Calgary: V. A. Wood, 1989), 93.

2. Melvin S. Tagg, "I Am Her Child," in Jack M. Lyon, Jay A. Parry, Linda R. Gundry, eds., *Best-Loved Stories of the LDS People*, vol. 2 (Salt Lake City: Deseret Book, 1999), 365.

UNIFYING TWO NATIONS

1. Richard and Bon Adell Skidmore, interview by author, audio recording, March 16, 2000.

PEACE AMID POLITICAL UNREST

1. Enrique O. Huerta, as cited in Jerry Johnston, "Worthy of the Heart of a People," *Church News*, May 13, 2000, 3.

DAD'S MILLENNIUM DAY LILIES

1. See David W. Martin and Ernie J. Shannon, "The Columbus Ohio Temple" (n.p., 1999), 55–56.
2. In ibid., 51–52.

TEMPERING THE WEATHER

1. Keith Brown, interview by author, audio recording, March 18, 2000.
2. Ibid.
3. Ibid.

A SPECIAL DREAM

1. Richard Gieseke, in Nielsen and Johnson, *Gift of Love—The Houston Texas Temple*, 90.
2. Ibid., 92.
3. Ibid., 93.

THE CRANE THAT ALMOST TOPPLED

1. In Esther Stratton's unpublished transcripts of testimonies from Kona Hawaii Temple workers, copy in author's possession, used by permission.

A SHIPWRECK AND SALVAGED LUMBER

1. See Hyrum C. Pope, "About the Temple in Hawaii," *Improvement Era* 23, no. 2 (1919); Richard O. Cowan, *Temples to Dot the Earth* (Salt Lake City: Bookcraft, 1989), 129–30.

2. See Joseph H. Spurrier, "The Hawaii Temple: A Special Place in a Special Land," paper presented at the seventh annual conference of the Mormon Pacific Historical Society, Laie, Hawaii, March 1, 1986, 33.

PRESIDENT TAYLOR AND THE SPIRIT OF DISCERNMENT

1. In Lundwall, *Temples of the Most High*, 100.
2. John Taylor, in ibid., 101.

FLOWERING OF FAITH

1. Aubrey Conner, in Nielsen and Johnson, *Gift of Love—The Houston Texas Temple*, 82.

AN INTERNATIONALLY DIVERSE TEMPLE

1. See Alison Beard, "All the Rage in New York," *Financial Times*, June 1, 2004.
2. Brent M. Cederlof, interview by author, audio recording, October 15, 2005.
3. Ibid.

A SAVING DREAM

1. See *The Manti Temple* (Manti, Utah: Manti Temple Centennial Committee, 1988), 24–25.
2. See ibid., 104.

PRESERVED DURING AN EARTHQUAKE

1. John Jay Erekson, interview by author, audio recording, September 26, 2000.

LAND PRESERVED FOR A TEMPLE

1. Lowell L. Cheney, "Miracles of the Bismarck North Dakota Temple Site," copy in cornerstone of Bismarck North Dakota Temple.

ROCKS OF FAITH

1. Jerry Quinn and Libby Quinn, temple construction missionaries, correspondence with author.
2. Vernon Forbush, interview by author, audio recording, June 3, 2005.

INDEX

INDEX

INDEX

INDEX

INDEX

INDEX

NOTES

A Most Sacred Experience

1. In N. B. Lundwall, *Temples of the Most High* (Salt Lake City: Bookcraft, 1993), 40.
2. Ibid., 141.

A Change of Heart

1. Rita Jensen, interview by author, audio recording, April 29, 2004.

Carjacked and Kidnapped

1. Adapted from Richard Lynn Higginson, unpublished personal history, copy in author's possession, used by permission.
2. Stratton, interview.

A Beacon in the Hurricane

1. See "Hurricane Wreaks Ruin in Samoa," *Church News*, December 21, 1991, Z3.
2. "Church Responds Swiftly to Samoa Disaster," *Church News*, December 28, 1991, Z14.

Many Hands Make Light Work

1. Weldon Smith, interview by author, audio recording, September 12, 2000.

Petitioning for a Temple

1. Susan Smith, in Joan R. Larsen, "History of the Billings Temple District," unpublished, 1999.
2. Gale Mair, Billings Montana Temple project superintendent, interview by author, audio recording, April 12, 2000.

The First Presidency and a Fire Chief

1. Ronald W. Thurber, interview by author, audio recording, September 26, 2000.
2. Ibid.

"I Am Her Child"

1. Heber J. Grant, as cited in V. A. Wood, *The Alberta Temple: Centre and Symbol of Faith* (Calgary: V. A. Wood, 1989), 93.

NOTES

2. Melvin S. Tagg, "I Am Her Child," in Jack M. Lyon, Jay A. Parry, Linda R. Gundry, eds., *Best-Loved Stories of the LDS People*, vol. 2 (Salt Lake City: Deseret Book, 1999), 365.

UNIFYING TWO NATIONS

1. Richard and Bon Adell Skidmore, interview by author, audio recording, March 16, 2000.

PEACE AMID POLITICAL UNREST

1. Enrique O. Huerta, as cited in Jerry Johnston, "Worthy of the Heart of a People," *Church News*, May 13, 2000, 3.

DAD'S MILLENNIUM DAY LILIES

1. See David W. Martin and Ernie J. Shannon, "The Columbus Ohio Temple" (n.p., 1999), 55–56.

2. In ibid., 51–52.

TEMPERING THE WEATHER

1. Keith Brown, interview by author, audio recording, March 18, 2000.

2. Ibid.

3. Ibid.

A SPECIAL DREAM

1. Richard Gieseke, in Nielsen and Johnson, *Gift of Love—The Houston Texas Temple*, 90.

2. Ibid., 92.

3. Ibid., 93.

THE CRANE THAT ALMOST TOPPLED

1. In Esther Stratton's unpublished transcripts of testimonies from Kona Hawaii Temple workers, copy in author's possession, used by permission.

A SHIPWRECK AND SALVAGED LUMBER

1. See Hyrum C. Pope, "About the Temple in Hawaii," *Improvement Era* 23, no. 2 (1919); Richard O. Cowan, *Temples to Dot the Earth* (Salt Lake City: Bookcraft, 1989), 129–30.